Enid Blyton

MORE ABOUT AMELIA JANE!

More Enid Blyton published by Dean

Amelia Jane Again!
Naughty Amelia Jane!
Good Idea, Amelia Jane!

Five O'Clock Tales
Six O'Clock Tales
Seven O'Clock Tales
Eight O'Clock Tales
The Enchanted Wood
The Folk of the Faraway Tree
The Magic Faraway Tree
Adventures of the Wishing Chair
The Wishing Chair Again
More Wishing Chair Stories

The Mystery of the Burnt Cottage
The Mystery of the Disappearing Cat
The Mystery of the Secret Room
The Mystery of the Spiteful Letters
The Mystery of the Missing Necklace
The Mystery of the Hidden House
The Mystery of the Pantomine Cat
The Mystery of the Invisible Thief
The Mystery of the Vanished Prince
The Mystery of the Strange Bundle
The Mystery of Holly Lane
The Mystery of Tally Ho Cottage
The Mystery of the Missing Man
The Mystery of the Strange Messages
The Mystery of Banshee Towers

First Term at Malory Towers
Second Form at Malory Towers
Third Year at Malory Towers
Upper Fourth at Malory Towers
In the Fifth at Malory Towers
Last Term at Malory Towers

Enid Blyton

MORE ABOUT AMELIA JANE!

DEAN

EGMONT

We bring stories to life

First published in Great Britain 1954 by Newnes
This edition published 2005 by Dean,
an imprint of Egmont Books Limited.
239 Kensington High Street, London W8 6SA

Text copyright © 1954 Enid Blyton Ltd
Illustrations copyright © 2005 Enid Blyton Ltd
Illustrations by Deborah Allwright

Enid Blyton's signature is a registered
trademark of Enid Blyton Limited.
A Chorion company

ISBN 0 6035 6192 6

1 3 5 7 9 10 8 6 4 2

A CIP catalogue record for this title is available from the British Library

Printed and bound in Singapore

Contents

Amelia Jane's Necklace   1

Amelia Jane and the Ink   22

Amelia Jane's Boomerang   37

Amelia Jane and the Scribbles   49

Amelia Jane Plays Postman   63

Amelia Jane is Naughty Again   77

Amelia Jane Goes Up the Tree   100

Amelia Jane and the Telephone   119

Now Then, Amelia Jane!   141

Amelia Jane Gets Into Trouble   157

Amelia Jane Has a Good Idea   176

Amelia Jane is Very Busy   197

Oh, Bother Amelia Jane!   212

Goodbye, Amelia Jane!   231

Amelia Jane's Necklace

You remember Amelia Jane, don't you, the naughty doll who lives in the nursery with Tom the toy soldier and the teddy bear and all the other toys?

She's still there – and still naughty, though she does sometimes turn over a new leaf. But, as Tom says, it's never a

very *big* leaf, and doesn't seem to last
long.

Now, one day Tom went exploring in
the toy-cupboard, and he found an old
cardboard box. It rattled when he shook
it, and he wondered what could be inside.

'Open it and see,' said the teddy bear. So Tom opened it. He and the bear stared at what was inside. They didn't at all know what the little brown things there were.

'Are they nice big beads?' said Tom.

'They might be something to eat,' said the bear, but he couldn't even nibble a hole in one of the smooth brown things.

The sailor doll strolled up to look. 'Oh, they are *acorns*,' he said. 'Didn't you know *that*?'

'What are acorns?' asked Tom, who had never heard of them in his life.

The sailor doll didn't know, but he pretended to. 'Oh, they are things that can be used for a bead necklace,' he said, remembering that he had once seen the children stringing them together. 'Yes, acorn beads, I suppose. They would make quite a nice necklace, wouldn't they?'

'Oh,' said the bear suddenly. 'Tom, do you think *I* might have an acorn necklace to wear round my neck? Ever since I lost my blue bow I've felt very cold about my neck. I should so like a necklace. It would keep my neck very warm.'

'Well, Teddy, we'll thread you one,' said Tom, who was always very kind. 'Now let me see – what do we want for threading beads?'

'A sharp needle – and some string,' said the sailor doll. 'Look – somebody has already made holes through the acorns, ready for threading. They must have done that and then forgotten all about them.'

Amelia Jane came up, full of curiosity. 'What's that you've got?' she said.

'Acorns,' said Tom, and turned away. He wasn't pleased with Amelia Jane. She had knocked his hat off that morning and pulled out a tuft of his hair to make whiskers for another toy.

'Acorns! What are they?' said Amelia.

'BEADS!' said the sailor doll. 'But

NOT for you. For the teddy bear, because he's lost his blue bow.'

'Well, I've lost the lace out of my shoes,' said Amelia Jane. 'I don't see why I shouldn't have the beads as much as the bear.'

'What's losing a shoe-lace got to do with having a necklace?' asked Tom.

'Quite a lot,' said Amelia, who could always argue for hours. 'You see, if I can't have a shoe-lace, I might as well have a neck-lace.'

'Don't be silly,' said the bear. 'You always want everything. Well, you're not going to have *this*!'

The sailor doll, the bear and the toy soldier took the box of acorn beads

away to a corner.
Amelia Jane
followed them.
They
wondered
where to get a
needle and
thread.

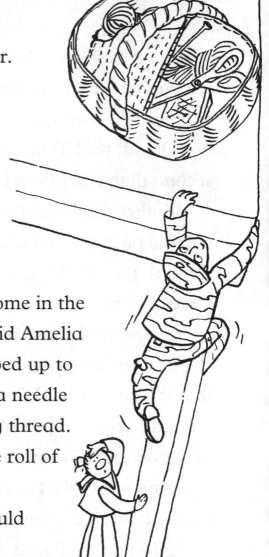

'There are some in the
work-basket,' said Amelia
Jane. Tom climbed up to
the table to get a needle
and some strong thread.
He found a little roll of
string there and
decided that would
do nicely.

Down he came. But, of course, nobody could thread the little needle with the thick string.

'Oooh!' said Tom. 'That's the second time I've pricked myself.'

'Bother this,' said the bear, trying hard to push the end of the string through the needle eye. 'It won't go. Oh dear – now *I've* pricked myself!'

'Let *me* try,' said Amelia Jane, and she took up the string. She saw at once that it wouldn't go through the eye of the little needle. She looked at the holes in the acorns. They were big – quite big enough to take the string without a needle to drag it through.

'*I'll* show you!' said Amelia, and

she picked up an acorn in her left hand. She ran the string through the hole in it and then picked up another.

'See? Quite easy! You are always so stupid. I'll thread the whole lot now.'

She threaded all the acorns very quickly. She really was clever at things like that.

'Thanks,' said Tom, when she had threaded the whole lot. 'That's fine. Now I'll put the necklace round the bear's neck. It will suit him.'

But Amelia Jane put it round her own! And what is more, she tied the string very tightly into a firm knot. She grinned round at the toys. 'It's mine!' she said, touching the necklace. 'I threaded it, didn't I?'

Well, what was to be done about *that*? Tom was so cross that he held Amelia Jane's arms, whilst the sailor doll tried to undo the knot of the necklace. But he couldn't possibly, because it was much too tight. So they had to give it up and marched off to the toy-cupboard very crossly indeed.

'Mean thing! She's always doing things like that,' said the bear. 'And I did so want a necklace for my throat, now I've lost my blue bow. I do feel upset.'

'It's just like Amelia Jane,' said the sailor doll, gloomily. 'Why didn't we think of her putting it on as soon as she'd finished it? Now we shall never have it, and she'll keep on and on saying, "Look at my beautiful new necklace!"'

That is just what Amelia Jane did say, of course! Whenever anyone came to visit the toys, she would show them her necklace. 'Isn't it lovely?' she would say. 'It's made of acorns. I've heard that they are very, very precious. I made this necklace all by myself!'

Now, that summer was very, very hot. The nursery children went away to the sea, and the toys were left by themselves in the nursery.

'I can't stand this heat,' said Amelia Jane, one day. 'I'm going out into the garden – and I'm going to undress and get into the pond to cool myself. It's no use saying I mustn't, because I'm GOING to!'

Well, she did, of course. She took off all her clothes except her underwear, which was sewn on and wouldn't come off, and she got into the water at the edge of the garden pond. She lay right down in it, with her head against the edge of the pond, and kicked and splashed in joy.

'It's lovely! It's so cold!' she called. 'Come along and enjoy yourselves, toys! Ooooh! This is delicious!'

The other toys paddled. They were afraid of undressing and getting right

into the water in case somebody came in
quickly and didn't give them time to
dress and get back to the toy-cupboard.
But Amelia Jane never cared about
things like that.

She spent all day in the water, and
the next day, too, lying there in her

underwear and acorn necklace, enjoying herself thoroughly. She frightened the sparrows who came to bathe, and she splashed the freckled thrush when he flew down. She really was full of mischief those hot, summer days, and soon no toy liked to go near the pond for fear of being soaked to the skin by Amelia Jane.

Now, if acorns are soaked in water for hours and hours they begin to grow! An acorn is the seed of an oak tree, and if it is made damp, it wants to put out a root and a shoot, like all seeds.

And Amelia Jane's acorns were no different from any other acorns. When they felt the water round them, soaking into them, they rejoiced, and grew fat. They wanted to burst their skins, and put out little white roots and shoots, to grow into tiny oak-trees!

Nobody noticed that the acorns had grown fat. Amelia Jane didn't, of course, because nobody can see what is tightly threaded round their neck. But when the acorns burst their skins a little, and put out white roots, Tom saw them, and gave a scream.

'What's the matter?' said the bear.

Tom pointed to Amelia Jane's neck. 'Look! Her necklace is growing white worms! Ugh, how horrible. Worms down her neck!'

Everyone stared at Amelia Jane's neck. She didn't like it at all. 'What's the matter?' she said. 'What's all this about worms?'

'Oh, Amelia Jane – it's quite true. Your necklace has got white worms in it,' said the sailor doll. 'They are wriggling out of the acorns. That's where they live, I suppose! Oooh, how horrible!'

'I don't believe you,' said Amelia, and she put up her hand to her necklace. She touched one or two of the growing white roots and gave a scream. 'Oh, I touched a worm! I did, I did! Oh, whatever shall I do?'

'Well, you *would* take the necklace,'

said the bear, quite pleased. 'It's your own fault. You shouldn't have been so selfish.'

Amelia Jane stood trembling in the nursery. 'Will they crawl down my neck?' she said, looking pale.

'I expect so,' said the bear, who was quite enjoying himself. 'If I were a worm I'd crawl all over you.'

Amelia screamed again. 'Don't! I can't bear it. Take them away! Undo my necklace, quick!'

'Certainly not,' said the sailor doll.

'You wanted to wear it, and you jolly well can!'

'I'll undo it myself,' said Amelia, but she couldn't. That knot was tied so tightly that she couldn't possibly undo it herself. And nobody else would.

'You can go on wearing worms,' said the bear. 'Fancy wearing a worm necklace! Ha, ha! It suits you, Amelia.'

'Please, please do untie the knot,' begged the big doll. 'Where are the scissors? We can cut the string.'

But there were no scissors to be

found. The work-basket had gone, and not one of the toys had any scissors of their own. So Amelia had to go on wearing her peculiar necklace.

She was very, very miserable. The toys watched the 'worms' growing longer each day, as the roots pushed out from the acorns. 'They're getting bigger, Amelia,' said the bear. 'And longer. And fatter. Oooooh! I wonder if those worms will get hungry, Amelia Jane, and nibble you.'

Amelia sobbed with fright. What could she do? The toy soldier was sorry for her and tried to undo the knot, but he couldn't. 'Go out into the garden and see if the worms will drop down and join the brown worms in the grass,' he said.

So Amelia went out and stood in the garden. And whilst she was there the string, which had got rather wet and rotten at the front of her neck, suddenly broke. And down fell all the acorns, with their funny white roots and tiny shoots.

'They've gone!' yelled Amelia, and fled indoors. The toys went out to see. There lay the acorns, with the white 'worms' sticking out of them.

'Let's bury them in the ground, then perhaps these white worms will go and join their brother brown worms,' said the sailor doll.

So they dug little holes and put the split acorns, with their roots and shoots, carefully in the earth.

And, would you believe it, they all grew into tiny little oak-trees, with strong, white roots delving deep into the ground, and little shoots that bore leaves in the sunshine!

But Amelia Jane didn't know that. She never went near that part of the garden, in case those white worms saw her and went after her.

Poor Amelia! She says she is never going to wear a necklace again, and I don't expect she ever will. The bear says it serves her right – but it really was very funny, wasn't it?

Amelia Jane and the Ink

Amelia Jane was in a very bad mood, and when Tom the toy soldier asked her to play with him, she pushed him away and started to quarrel with him.

'You can't play games,' Amelia Jane shouted. 'You are so stupid.'

'I'm not stupid,' said Tom.

'Yes, you are,' said Amelia Jane.

'Stop it, you two,' said the bear. 'Don't take any notice of Amelia Jane, Tom.'

'It's difficult not to,' said Tom.

The toys began to talk together, but they wouldn't talk to Amelia. When she was in one of her silly moods, they just took no notice of her.

She didn't like that. 'Be quiet, stop talking,' she said. 'I'm going to write a letter.'

'Well, write it. We don't care!' said the bear. 'Who are you going to write it to?'

'Father Christmas,' said Amelia.

'Well, tell him to come and take you away and put you in his sack, and pop you into a stocking in some other nursery,' said Tom.

Amelia Jane was angry. 'You're unkind,' she said. 'I shall write to him – but I shall ask him to come and take *you* away. So there. You'll be sorry you were nasty to me, then.'

Tom felt rather frightened. He wasn't

at all sure that Father Christmas might not do what Amelia said.

'Father Christmas never reads any letters unless they are written in ink,' he said at last. He knew Amelia Jane only had a pencil to write with.

She looked at him. He said it so loudly that she thought it must be true. 'All right!' she said. 'I'll write my letter in ink then!'

The toys stared at her in horror. Not even the children in the nursery were allowed to write in ink. Their mother said they were not old enough. So the ink was always kept out of reach on the mantelpiece.

'Amelia Jane! You'd never dare to

write in *ink*!' said the bear.

'Wouldn't I?' said Amelia. 'Well, you just see! I shall write my letter in ink, with a pen, and I shall blot it properly and everything.'

'You can't reach the ink,' said the bear.

'I can,' said Amelia.

'You're not to,' said the clockwork clown.

'I just shall then,' said Amelia. She went to the coal-scuttle and climbed up on top of it. From there she climbed on to the top of the nursery fireguard, which went all round the hearth.

Then she leaned on the mantelpiece to try and reach the bottle of ink.

She just could!

She edged it carefully towards her.
Then she took the bottle into her hands.
'I've got it!' she cried. 'Look!'
She turned to show the toys – and
lost her balance! She fell off the guard

on to the hearth-rug – bump! The bottle
of ink flew into the air and then fell bang
on to Amelia's head. Its cork shot out
and the ink poured all over Amelia's
face! Some went into her mouth. She
spat it out at once.

'Poof! It's horrid!'

The toys stared at Amelia Jane in horror. Her face was blue all over. She did look funny. The toys didn't like her at all. She didn't look like Amelia Jane. She looked rather fierce and wild.

'What's the matter?' said Amelia Jane, as the toys began to edge away from her.

'We don't like you. You're all blue in the face now,' said the bear.

'As blue as the sailor doll's trousers,' said Tom.

'You frighten me!' squealed the clockwork mouse, and raced into the toy-cupboard as if a cat were after him.

'Don't be silly,' said Amelia, trying to wipe her face with her hand. It made her hand blue. She stared at it and wondered what she looked like. There was a mirror over the book-case. Amelia Jane pushed a chair by the book-case, climbed up it and stood on the top of the book-case. She looked at herself in the mirror there.

'Oh! Oh!' she squealed. 'It isn't me!

It isn't me! I'm somebody else! Oh, where have I gone? It isn't me!'

The toys looked at her. Certainly Amelia Jane didn't look like herself at all.

'There's only one thing to do, Amelia,' said Tom. 'You'll have to scrub your face!'

'Yes, I will, I will,' sobbed poor Amelia, taking another look at herself in the mirror, and then scrambling quickly down to the floor. 'Tom, get a scrubbing-brush, quick.'

Tom went to the basin and climbed up on to the chair below. He knew there was a nail-brush there. He took it and rubbed it on the soap. Then he climbed down and went to Amelia Jane.

'Shall I do the scrubbing?' he asked. Amelia nodded. So Tom began to scrub her face. How he scrubbed!

'The soap's gone in my eye!' yelled Amelia Jane. Tom took no notice.

'Now it's in the other eye!' sobbed Amelia. 'Don't scrub so hard.'

Tom went on scrubbing. 'You're scrubbing my face away,' wailed poor Amelia. 'Don't scrub my nose so hard. Oh, it'll come off, I know it will!'

All the toys stood round, grinning. They couldn't help thinking that it was a very good punishment for Amelia Jane, after quarrelling with Tom so much, and trying to take the ink.

How he scrubbed! Amelia sobbed
and cried, and her eyes smarted with the
soap, but Tom wouldn't stop until her
face was perfectly clean again. All the

toys cheered him on. At last his arm ached and he put down the nail-brush.

'There,' he said, 'now you're all right.'

'Thank you,' sobbed Amelia. 'Oh dear, oh dear, why ever did I say I'd write in ink? Look at the mess on the hearthrug!'

Poor Amelia had to set to work and scrub that clean too. She put the empty bottle of ink back on the mantelpiece, feeling very guilty.

'You ought to look in your money-box and put some money by the bottle to pay for some more ink,' said the bear.

So Amelia looked in her money-box and put five coins on the mantelpiece by the bottle. The children found them there the next day, and they *were* surprised!

'Where did this money come from?' they wondered, and they turned to look at the toys. 'Goodness – isn't Amelia's face clean! Whatever has happened to it?'

They might have guessed when they found that their nail-brush was blue with ink – but they didn't!

As for Amelia Jane, she told Tom she was sorry she had quarrelled with him – so one good thing came out of her naughty prank, after all!

Amelia Jane's Boomerang

Amelia Jane found a toy boomerang at the back of the cupboard. Do you know what a boomerang is? It is a bit of curved wood made in such a way that it will always come back to the one who throws it.

You can see the boomerang Amelia Jane found if you look at the picture. She didn't know what it was, at first. Then, when she threw it into the air and found that it came back to her, she was thrilled.

'Now I'll have some fun!' she cried, and she threw the boomerang at the chimneys on the dolls' house! It knocked them off and they slid down the roof, fell to the ground and gave the clockwork mouse a terrible fright.

The boomerang flew back to Amelia Jane, and she caught it. 'Now I'll take off the sailor doll's hat!' she said with a giggle, and threw it again. It neatly took off the sailor doll's hat, and came back to Amelia Jane. She laughed at the sailor doll's look of surprise when he felt

his hat knocked off.

'Oh, my goodness! Amelia Jane
has found the old boomerang!' said
the bear. 'I hid it away. Amelia, give
it to me.'

Amelia Jane threw the
boomerang at him, and it sliced off
the tip of one of his ears, and then
flew back to the doll. The bear
was very angry.

He ran at Amelia to get the boomerang. But she flung it at him again and he fell over. The boomerang returned to her hand. She laughed excitedly.

'It's no good! I'm *awfully* good with this. If you come rushing at me I'll throw it at you. So keep away. Now watch – I'm going to throw it at the snapdragons in that vase! I'll chop off some of their heads!'

And that's just what she did! The boomerang flew through the air, hit two snapdragons, broke their pretty heads, and then came flying back to the naughty doll.

Amelia Jane had a lovely time that

day. She knocked the little china dog off the mantelpiece with her boomerang and he fell on to the hearth and broke a bit off one paw. She threw it at the little mouse who came for crumbs, and he lost two of his whiskers. And she threw it at the railway train and cut the funnel right off.

'How can we stop it?' said the clockwork clown in despair. He had had his hat knocked off six times by the boomerang and now he had stuffed it into his pocket for safety.

'I know where the old pop-gun is,' said the pink cat suddenly. 'Shall we get that? It's got a cork on a string, and it always jerks back when it's shot out. You

 put the cork into the
end of the gun, press
the trigger – and out
shoots the cork. But
because it's on a
string it always jerks
back to the shooter
again, like the boomerang goes back to
Amelia Jane.'

This was quite a long speech for the
pink cat to make, and everyone listened
to it, except Amelia Jane, who was
trying to knock down a silver thimble left
on the mantelpiece.

'Yes! Get the pop-gun!' cried the
bear, so the pink cat went to get it. He
brought it out of an old box and showed

it to the others. Tom the toy soldier fitted the cork into the end. It was on a long string tied to the gun. He pressed the trigger.

POP! Out flew the cork quite fiercely, and hit the bear on the right paw. He gave a yell. 'Don't practise on me, silly! That stung! Practise on Amelia Jane!'

Tom grinned. He went over to Amelia Jane and pointed the pop-gun at the back of her head.

POP! The cork flew out, caught her hair-ribbon, and then jerked back on its string.

Amelia Jane got a terrible shock.

'Oh! What was that?' she cried, and swung round at once.

'We've got a boomerang-cork!' grinned Tom, and shot at her again. POP! The cork hit her on the nose, and she almost fell over.

'Now you stop that!' cried Amelia Jane, 'or I'll throw my boomerang at you!'

'Well, every time you throw your boomerang we're going to shoot you with the pop-gun!' said Tom, putting the cork into the gun again. 'There's no reason why we shouldn't have a bit of fun, too! Look out!'

Pop! The cork hit Amelia Jane right in her middle and she gave a squeal. 'Oh! Oh! You've hit my dinner! Wait till I get that horrid cork! I'll throw it away!'

But she couldn't get the cork because it was tied on with string to the gun, and it always jerked back when it was fired out.

The toys had a wonderful time chasing her round the nursery, popping the cork at her. She didn't have a chance to throw the boomerang at them.

'You're very unkind,' she sobbed as she tried to dodge the toys.

'Oh, no – we're only doing the sort of

thing you've been doing,' said Tom. 'You give us your boomerang and we'll give you the pop-gun. Then we can each have a turn at throwing the boomerang too.'

'No,' said Amelia. 'You'd only throw that at me as well. Promise not to and I'll give it to you.'

They promised, and Amelia Jane handed over the boomerang. Tom at once went to hide it away where it would never be found again. But, oh dear, Amelia Jane didn't promise not to shoot at the toys with the pop-gun, and the very first thing she did was to point it at the bear and fire.

POP! It flew out and hit him so hard

in his tummy that it made him growl. But she couldn't shoot the cork again because Tom had cut the string and it didn't jerk back to the gun!

'Aha!' said the sailor doll, picking up the loose cork and putting it into his pocket, 'you won't do *that* again, naughty Amelia Jane! Go and stand in the corner till we say you can come out. If you don't,

we'll take the gun, tie on the string to the cork and do a bit of shooting again!'

So Amelia Jane is standing in the corner, sulking, and I rather think the toys are going to forget about her for a very long time!

Amelia Jane and the Scribbles

One day Amelia Jane found a red pencil on the floor. Somebody had dropped it there and forgotten to pick it up. Amelia Jane was pleased.

'Now I can write things in red,' she said. 'Look, this is a pencil that writes in red, toys.'

'Well, if you think you're going to

write in my notebook, you're wrong,' said Tom.

'And if you think I'm going to lend you my little drawing-book to scribble in, you can think again,' said the teddy bear.

'And don't you dare to scribble inside the lid of the brick-box,' said the clockwork clown. 'I spent ages rubbing out some silly scribbles the pink cat did once with a bit of coal.'

'I don't know why you're so sharp with me,' said Amelia Jane. 'Anyone would think I wanted to do something naughty.'

'It's not at all surprising that we should think that,' said the bear. 'You've been fairly good for about a week. That's about as long as you *can* be good for.'

Amelia Jane badly wanted to scribble with her red pencil, but nobody would lend her any paper at all. So she got cross and went inside the toy-cupboard all by herself. When she came out, she was smiling.

'Now, what's she smiling like that for?' said Tom, and he went inside the toy-cupboard. He gave an angry cry, and the toys went to see why.

'Look!' he said, pointing to the wall at the back of the cupboard. 'Look what she's done.'

The toys looked. Written across the wall were lots of words: '*The toy soldier is silly. The teddy bear is too fat. The clockwork clown is clumsy. The clockwork mouse is a baby.*'

'Look at that!' said the clown. 'How disgraceful! Doesn't Amelia Jane know that no decent people ever scribble on walls? Only the very lowest toys do that!'

They went to find Amelia, but they couldn't. But they found something scribbled on the wall near the toy-cupboard, at the bottom:

'*You're all sillies! I shall do what I like, so there! Signed, Amelia Jane.*'

'Isn't she awful?' said the bear. 'Now we shall have to spend ages rubbing this out before anyone sees it. Go and borrow some dusters from the dolls in the dolls' house, Tom.'

But when he got to the dolls' house, he found all the small dolls in a very bad temper.

'Somebody's been in and scribbled over our walls,' said Dinah, the mother doll. 'Look. Someone's written: "*This is a silly dolls' house.*'"

'What a shame,' said the bear. 'That's Amelia Jane. She wants scribbling on herself!'

'That's an awfully good idea of yours, bear,' said the clown. 'If only we could! That would soon stop her silly tricks!'

'Listen,' said the bear, thinking out a plan. 'We're giving a party tomorrow night, aren't we, to all the pixies who live in the garden outside? Well, let's wait till Amelia Jane is asleep tonight, and we'll scribble something across her forehead! She won't know, because she hardly ever looks at herself in the mirror, even to do her hair.'

All the toys giggled. That would be a good joke! They spent quite a lot of time rubbing out the things Amelia Jane had scribbled everywhere, and the big doll peeped out from behind the curtain, and laughed. She didn't know what they were planning for her, or she would have been on her guard.

That night Amelia Jane climbed up into one of the dolls' cots and lay down to sleep. She felt tired. She had done such a lot of writing that day! The toys waited till she was fast asleep, and then Tom climbed up softly to the cot. He sat down gently beside Amelia Jane.

'Pass me the paint-box,' he

whispered, and the bear passed it up. A
bright red colour was already mixed
for him, and the paint-brush was there
as well.

Tom began to paint words quickly
on Amelia Jane's big smooth forehead.
'*This is naughty Amelia Jane*' he put,
and tried not to giggle.

Amelia Jane thought it was a fly walking over her head when she felt the paint-brush in her sleep. 'Go away, fly,' she murmured, and that made Tom almost laugh out loud.

He slid down to the floor when he had finished. He wouldn't let the others go up and see what he had done, in case they wakened Amelia Jane. 'Wait till she wakes,' he said. 'Oh, won't it be funny at the party? We shan't need to introduce Amelia Jane to anyone! They'll only have to read what's on her forehead!'

Well, it *was* funny! The pixie guests came along in crowds, longing to dance to the music of the musical-box and to eat the little cakes that Dinah had cooked on the dolls'-house stove. The bear was the host, and he introduced everyone.

But he didn't need to say who Amelia Jane was because as soon as the guests saw her they all giggled and said: 'Oh, this is naughty Amelia Jane!'

Amelia Jane was surprised and cross. She didn't like being called naughty at a party. She frowned and sulked. But as soon as everyone came up to her, the same thing was said: 'Oh, this is naughty Amelia Jane!'

'Why do you say that?' said Amelia, crossly, and she frowned so hard that she wrinkled up all the red words on her forehead.

'Don't do that – we can't read your name!' said a small pixie. Amelia Jane stared at him.

'What do you mean, you can't read my name? Of course you can't. Don't be silly.'

'Oh, now I can,' said the little pixie, when Amelia had stopped frowning. 'Yes – this is naughty Amelia Jane.'

Amelia Jane went to the teddy bear, almost crying. 'Why is everyone horrid to me? Why do they keep saying, "This is naughty Amelia Jane"? Tell me.'

'No,' said the bear.

'Yes,' said Amelia. 'I want to know, please, please, bear.'

'I'll tell you if you promise to give me that red pencil and never to scribble anywhere again,' said the bear. 'It's a low thing to do.'

'All right,' said Amelia Jane, with a sigh. 'I won't scribble any more. Here's the pencil.'

'Thanks. Now go and look at yourself in the mirror,' said the bear, and Amelia went.

She screamed when she saw the red words on her forehead. 'Oh! Oh, how mean! Now I know why everyone said what they did. I shan't go back to the party.'

So she didn't. She stayed and moped in the toy-cupboard, and that's where the bear found her halfway through. 'Come along,' he said. 'Come and dance.'

'No,' said Amelia. 'Not with this horrid scribble on my forehead.'

The bear took out his hanky. 'Lick

it,' he said to Amelia Jane, and she licked his hanky. He rubbed the licky bit over her forehead.

'There!' he said. 'The scribble's gone. Now come along and dance – and mind you behave yourself, or I might write something else on you. You never know!'

So Amelia Jane behaved herself. But I'm afraid her good behaviour won't last long!

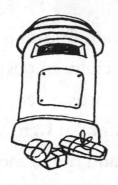

Amelia Jane
Plays Postman

I really must tell you the latest story
about Amelia Jane.

On the nursery mantelpiece stood a
money-box. It looked exactly like a
pillar-box, and it was painted red just
like the big ones we post letters in down
the road.

But instead of posting letters in their box the children posted money, of course, and it was a very good way of saving it. 'Clink!' it went when it was dropped in, and the money-box grew heavier and heavier.

Mother kept the key of the box and only unlocked it when the children wanted to take out some money to buy someone a birthday present. She unlocked the box at the bottom then, and the children took the money out.

Now, Amelia Jane suddenly took it into her head that if she found anything left about by the toys she would post it in the red money-box on the mantelpiece! That made the toys very angry indeed.

'Amelia Jane! Have you taken my pink ribbon?' cried the bear.

'Yes. And I've posted it,' said Amelia. 'You are getting very untidy, Teddy, leaving your things about. It will teach you to be tidy.'

Teddy was furious, of course. And so was the clockwork clown when he found that Amelia had actually posted the button that came off his trousers.

'How dare you do that?' he shouted. 'I couldn't help it coming off, could I? I know somebody would have sewn it on again, if you hadn't picked it up and posted it. You're SILLY, Amelia Jane!'

And then she posted the toy soldier's belt! It was a bit tight, so he had undone it and had just put it down while he straightened his trousers a little, when Amelia Jane pounced on it. He was too late to get it back! Into the red money-box it went.

'Now I haven't got a belt!' shouted Tom. 'I look awful.

Stop this nonsense, Amelia Jane, or we'll start posting *your* things in that box!'

'You can't,' said Amelia with a grin. 'I'm the only one that can reach the mantelpiece.'

This was quite true. Amelia Jane was a very big doll and a good climber too. She could reach up to the chair near the fireplace, climb over to the mantelpiece and climb on to that. Then it was easy to post anything in the money-box there.

But none of the other toys could get on to the mantelpiece, so they couldn't possibly post anything belonging to Amelia. It was most annoying. After she had posted the baby doll's dear little comb, the toys held a meeting. Amelia Jane was asleep in her chair, so she didn't hear a word.

'We've got to do *some*thing to stop her,' said the clock. 'She'll be posting the clockwork mouse's tail next!'

The mouse gave a squeal. 'No, no! Don't say that! I couldn't bear it.'

'How can we stop her?' wondered the baby doll.

The teddy bear suddenly slapped his plump knee.

'I know. I've got an idea!'

'Sh! Don't wake Amelia,' said the clown.

'Now listen,' said the teddy,

excitedly. 'You know next week it's the birthday of the little mouse who lives in the hole in the wall, don't you? Well, listen – ooooh, it's *such* a good idea – you see . . .'

'Oh, do go on! Do tell us!' said the clockwork mouse, impatiently.

'Well – we'll pretend that we are giving the little mouse all sorts of tiny presents, wrapped up in parcels,' said the teddy, grinning. '*But* – we'll put inside the parcels little things belonging to Amelia Jane! We'll put her best hair-ribbon in – and one of her Sunday shoes – and that brooch she likes so much – and her best sash . . .'

'But dear me, we can't *possibly* give

her things to the little mouse,' said Tom, shocked. 'That would be quite wrong.'

'Oh, don't you *see* what will happen?' said the teddy. 'Amelia Jane will find the parcels – and she won't be able to stop herself *posting* them – in the money-box! And she'll have posted all her own things and won't be able to get them back!'

There was a silence. Then the toys giggled and thumped Teddy on the back. 'You're marvellous!' they cried. 'It is a simply wonderful idea! We'll do it! Oh, how we'll laugh to see Amelia posting her own things!'

Well, they did just what they had

planned. They found Amelia's brooch and wrapped it up. They found her best sash, folded it neatly and wrapped it in paper and tied it with string. They took her hair-ribbon and did that up too, and one of her best shoes! Soon there were four neat little parcels at the back of the toy-cupboard.

And, of course, it wasn't long before Amelia Jane found them. 'Aha!' she said. 'I suppose these are birthday parcels for that silly little mouse who lives in the wall. I'll post them!'

71

'I warn you not to,' said Tom. 'You'll be sorry if you do, Amelia.'

Amelia laughed and picked up all the parcels. She went towards the fireplace to climb on the chair there.

'You have been warned!' called the clown. But Amelia took no notice at all. Ha – this was a fine trick to play on the toys – to post all the parcels they had got ready for the little mouse!

Thud, thud, thud, thud! Down into the money-box they went, and there they stayed. Amelia Jane climbed down, smiling. 'I have been warned!' she said, mockingly. 'But *I* don't care.'

Nobody said anything. They just waited in patience till Amelia wanted her brooch or her ribbon or sash. She soon did, because she was to go to a party given by the doll in the next house. The children were taking her.

'I shall wear my best shoes, my sash, my blue hair-ribbon, and my brooch,' she said. 'I *shall* look grand!'

But she couldn't find them, though she hunted everywhere. She turned to the watching toys. 'You know something about them!' she cried. 'What have you done with them?'

'Nothing – except just wrap them up into neat little parcels!' grinned the clown.

'But what for? Oh, *what's* happened to my precious, precious things?'

groaned Amelia.

'You should know,' said the bear. 'You picked up all the parcels yesterday.'

'You p-p-p-posted them!' squealed the clockwork mouse, stammering in excitement, and then going off into a fit of giggles.

'I *posted* them!' said Amelia. 'What do you mean? Those were birthday parcels for the mouse, weren't they? Oh, oh, oh – why didn't you tell me what they were?'

'We warned you, we did warn you not to post them,' said the clown, and he went off into giggles, too.

Amelia Jane cried bitterly. She

didn't go to the party.
She moped all day
long till the toys felt
quite sorry for
her. Then she
dried her
eyes.

'I'm
sorry I
posted everybody's things,' she said. 'I
know what it feels like now to lose my
things in that money-box. I'll find the
key, undo the box and get everything
out.'

But she couldn't find the key because
Mother had it in her purse. So
everything has got to stay there till

somebody has a birthday and the money-box is unlocked.

And *what* a surprise the children are going to get when they see all the things that Amelia Jane has posted! I'm sure the clockwork mouse will have a fit of the giggles again!

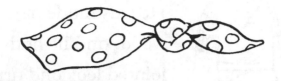

Amelia Jane is Naughty Again

Listen to what Amelia Jane did a little while ago – she's almost as rascally as Brer Rabbit sometimes!

It all happened when a new toy came to stay in the nursery. He really belonged to the children's cousin, but she was going away and asked her cousins to look after this toy for her.

He was rather a peculiar-looking toy. He was made of wood, and he had jointed legs and arms and hands – and even toes. He was dressed like a gardener, with a green baize apron in front, a scarf round his neck, and rolled-up sleeves that showed his jointed arms.

The peculiar thing about him was his head. It could nod up and down and shake from side to side because it was on a kind of spring. It was very surprising to the toys to see somebody that could nod his head or shake it like that.

'What's your name?' asked Amelia Jane. 'Do we call you Mr Noddy or Mr Shaky?'

'I've got a cousin called Mr Shaky,' said the wooden man. 'I'm called Mr Up-and-To.'

'What a peculiar name!' said the sailor doll.

'Not really,' said the wooden man. 'Just a mixture of *Up*-and-Down and *To*-and-Fro – Mr Up-and-To.'

'Why not Mr Fro-and-Down?' asked Amelia Jane, and went off into giggles.

'How clever you are!' said Mr Up-

and-To, admiringly. 'That's a *much* nicer name! Really, I think you are a very clever doll.'

'Oh, I am,' said Amelia Jane at once. 'Aren't I, toys? If anything goes wrong, ask me how to put it right! If you want to know anything, ask me! If you –'

'That's enough, Amelia Jane,' said Tom. 'Stop blowing your own trumpet.'

'Oh, can she blow a trumpet, too?' said Mr Up-and-To, surprised. 'Well, well – if that isn't cleverer still. My mouth's too wooden to hold a trumpet.'

'Amelia's mouth is big enough to

hold a dozen trumpets, if she wanted to blow them about herself,' said the bear.

'Don't be unkind,' said Amelia Jane. 'You know I'm very clever.'

'I know you're very, very naughty,' said the bear. 'Now, you leave Mr Up-and-To alone, and don't stuff him up with any more tales.'

But Amelia Jane wouldn't leave the little wooden man alone. For one thing, he really was very, very stupid, and he believed every word anyone said. Amelia Jane found that out at once, and, oh, the tricks she played on that poor wooden man!

'Don't go near the brick-box,' she

would say. 'It's Monday today, and there might be a snake there!'

And, will you believe it, Mr Up-and-To would keep right the other side of the nursery, afraid that a snake might spring out at him.

'Don't go too near the Noah's Ark today, because it's Friday,' Amelia would say next. 'The lions are always so fierce on Friday.'

Mr Up-and-To didn't go near the Noah's Ark all day long. He asked Amelia Jane why the lions were so fierce on Fridays.

'Well, I expect that's the day they're fed at the Zoo,' said Amelia Jane, and the poor stupid little wooden man thought that was a very good reason.

'You're bad, Amelia Jane,' said Tom. 'Stuffing him up with tales like that. Whatever will you say next?'

'Aha! You wait and see!' said Amelia. And she went and whispered in Mr Up-and-To's big wooden ear.

'Don't go near the toy soldier today because it's Saturday and he might bite you.'

Poor Mr Up-and-To! He ran away as soon as Tom came near, and as Amelia Jane had given Tom a sweet to take to the wooden man, he kept on trying to find him, so that he could give him the sweet.

'I can't *think* why the wooden man keeps rushing off as soon as he sees me,' said Tom, surprised.

'It's Saturday and he doesn't like soldiers on Saturday,' said Amelia Jane, wickedly.

'Don't be silly,' said Tom. 'Here, take your sweet back. I'm not going to

rush after Mr Up-and-To all day long. You've told him something about me. I know you!'

Now one day Amelia Jane put a knot into her little blue hanky to remind her not to forget to mend her dress. Mr Up-and-To saw her knotting the knot, and he was most interested.

'What's that for?' he asked.

'Well, most people put a knot into their hanky if they want to remember something,' said Amelia. 'This knot says to me: "Mend your dress tonight, Amelia Jane." And I shall.'

'Very, very clever,' said the wooden man. 'I think I shall do that too, Amelia. I'm always forgetting things, aren't I?'

'Well, you just try putting knots into your hanky, and you will soon have a marvellous memory,' said Amelia Jane.

So the next time Mr Up-and-To wanted to remember something, he took out his big, red-spotted hanky and tied a very large knot in it.

'That's to tell me to remember to clean my shoes tonight,' he said to himself. But, of course, when he saw the knot again he couldn't for the life of him remember what he had put it into his hanky for.

I'll ask Amelia Jane, he thought. She always knows everything. So he went to find the big doll.

'Amelia,' he said, 'supposing I forgot what I had put a knot in my hanky for, would you be able to tell me?'

'Of course!' said Amelia, with a very wicked grin.

'Well, what's this knot for?' asked the wooden man, and he showed her the very big knot.

'Oh – that's to remind you to climb up to the basin-taps with a jug from the dolls' house, fill it with water, and give me a drink,' said Amelia at once.

'Is it really?' said the wooden man, in surprise. 'Well, fancy me forgetting that! I'll go at once, Amelia Jane.'

So, much to the toys' amazement, he got a jug, climbed all the way up to the basin, and held the jug under the tap-drips till he got it full. Then he gave Amelia Jane a drink.

'Well! He must be very fond of her,' said the clockwork clown, in surprise. 'Fancy doing all that for *Amelia*!'

Amelia was pleased. Her naughty mind began to work hard – and the very next time Mr Up-and-To was asleep she crept up to him, took his hanky from his pocket and made a very big knot there!

So, of course, the next time he took it out another knot stared him in the face. What *could* it be for?

'Oh, that?' said Amelia Jane. 'Dear, dear, have you forgotten already why you put it there, Mr Up-and-To? Why, it was to remind you to go to the toy sweet shop and bring me six of those tiny pink sweets.'

'Dear me – was it really?' said Mr Up-and-To, puzzled. 'I simply can't remember that at all! But I'll go at once, Amelia Jane.'

So he solemnly went to the toy-shop and took six of the little pink sweets from a bottle and gave them to Amelia Jane. She popped them all into her mouth at once.

Tom and the bear came over in a hurry. They spoke very sternly to Mr Up-and-To.

'Look here! That's stealing. Those sweets belong to the children, not to us. How dare you! Put them back!'

'He can't,' said Amelia, speaking with her mouth full. 'I'm eating them.'

'Did she tell you to get them?' the bear asked the wooden man.

'Well, no – not exactly. I – er – I put a knot in my hanky to remember to get them,' said Mr Up-and-To. 'I must say I'm very surprised at myself for putting a knot there to remind me of that. I'm very, very sorry, Teddy.'

Amelia Jane giggled to herself. She felt very naughty indeed, with a nice stupid fellow like Mr Up-and-To to play tricks on.

She put more knots in his hanky, and when he asked her what they could possibly be for she told him all sorts of things.

'That knot you put there is to remind you to get me the little blue brooch you'll find in a box at the back of the toy-cupboard,' she said. It belonged to the baby doll, and it was very bad of Amelia Jane to get the wooden man to fetch it for her.

'And that knot's to remind you to get me some cakes from the dolls'-house kitchen,' said Amelia another time. 'They've been baking today. And look, there's a little tiny knot in this corner of your hanky – that's to tell you to remember to have a cake for yourself, too.'

And, dear me, there were Amelia

Jane and the wooden man both eating cakes together!

The toys were very, very angry, and the dolls'-house dolls threatened to fetch a policeman.

'If you tell Mr Up-and-To any more naughty things to do, we'll punish you, Amelia Jane,' said the bear. 'Oh, we know it's you all right! He's too stupid to think of these things himself. You put them into his head.'

Amelia got cross. She put *four* knots in Mr Up-and-To's hanky at once. He ran to her, most surprised, when he discovered them. 'Amelia Jane! Look here – I've put *four* knots this time. Whatever can they be for?'

'This one's to remind you to pull the toy soldier's nose, and this one's to remind you to tread on the tail of the clockwork mouse, and that's to tell you to be sure and pinch the teddy bear, and that's to remind you to run off with the clown's key,' said Amelia Jane.

Well, the wooden man was most astonished at himself. To think he had decided to do all those things and had actually put knots in his hanky to remind him. Well, well – he'd better start off with the toy soldier. He would pull his nose.

He tried to, but Tom caught his wooden hands, and stopped him.

'Listen, Mr Up-and-To,' he said sternly. 'What's up with you? You *seem* so gentle and good, and a bit stupid – and yet you do all kinds of very, very naughty things. Why?'

'It's the knots in my hanky,' explained the wooden man sadly. 'Amelia Jane always tells me what they're for, you see. She knows.'

The toys went off to the back of the toy-cupboard to have a meeting. So *that's* what Amelia Jane was doing!

'She puts the knots in the hanky when the old wooden man is asleep,' said Teddy. 'And then when he asks her what he's put them there for, she tells him all kinds of nonsense. Well – *I'm* going to tell him what his next knot is for!'

The toys grinned. They could guess what the bear was going to tell Mr Up-and-To.

It was the bear that night who put a knot into the wooden man's hanky. It was such an enormous knot that the hanky seemed all knot when he had finished!

Mr Up-and-To was astonished to see such a big knot when he woke up. The bear was just nearby, so instead of asking Amelia Jane he showed the knot to Teddy.

'Look at that!' he said. 'A tremendous knot. Something *most* important to remember. I'd better ask Amelia Jane what it is for.'

'No, don't,' said the bear. 'She wouldn't dream of telling you what the knot's for. Ask me – or the toy soldier – or the clown. We all know. We'll tell you all right.'

'Tell me then,' said the wooden man.

'That knot, that very large knot, is to remind you to be sure and give Amelia Jane a good scolding,' said the bear. 'Don't look so surprised. That's what the knot is there for. Isn't it, Tom? Isn't it, everyone?'

And all the toys nodded and said yes, that was what the very large knot meant.

'She's been bad to you,' said Teddy. 'She's tried to make you bad, too. She must be punished – and you are the one to punish her, Mr Up-and-To. Go now.'

So he's gone to find Amelia Jane, feeling very cross indeed. She tried to make him bad, did she? Mr Up-and-To didn't want to be bad. He'd give Amelia Jane a good scolding!

She's hiding, of course. But the wooden man will find her. He's very, very determined once he makes his mind up – and sooner or later there'll be howls from the nursery, I'm sure of that.

I don't feel a bit sorry, and neither does anyone else. Amelia Jane has had her fun, and now, alas, she's got to pay for it!

Amelia Jane Goes Up the Tree

It was springtime, and the birds were all nesting. Amelia Jane was most excited.

'The birds are building their nests,' she said. 'They are laying eggs.'

'Well, they do that every year,' said Tom.

'I want to make a collection of birds' eggs,' said Amelia Jane, grandly.

'You naughty doll!' said the clockwork clown. 'You know quite well you mustn't take birds' eggs.'

'Well, I don't see why birds can't spare me one or two of their eggs,' said Amelia. 'After all – they can't count.'

'Amelia Jane, you know quite well that birds get dreadfully upset if they see anyone near their nests,' said the teddy bear. 'You know that sometimes they get very frightened, and they desert their nests – leave them altogether – so that the eggs get cold, and never hatch out.'

'Oh, don't lecture me so!' said Amelia Jane. 'I said I wanted to make a collection of birds' eggs, and so I am going to. You can't stop me.'

'You are a very bad doll,' said the clown, and he turned his back on Amelia. 'I don't like you one bit.'

Amelia Jane laughed. She was feeling in a very naughty mood. She looked out of the window, down into a big chestnut tree. In the fork of a branch was a nest. It belonged to a thrush.

'There's a thrush's nest just down there,' said Amelia. 'I wish I could climb down. But I can't. It's too dangerous. Perhaps I could climb up.'

'How could you do that?' said the curly-haired doll, in a scornful voice. 'Don't be silly. None of us could climb up that tall trunk!'

But the next day Amelia Jane was excited. 'The gardener has put a ladder up the chestnut tree!' she said. 'He has, really. He is cutting off some of the bigger branches, because they knock against the low roof of the shed. I shall slip down, wait till the gardener has gone to his dinner, and then climb the ladder!'

'Amelia Jane! You don't mean to say you really *are* going to rob a bird's nest!' cried the clown.

'Oh yes,' said Amelia. 'Why should the bird mind if one or two eggs are taken? She will probably be glad that she hasn't so many hungry beaks to fill, when the eggs hatch out!'

So, to the horror of the watching toys, Amelia Jane slipped downstairs, out of the garden door and up to the ladder, as soon as the gardener had gone to his dinner.

The toys all pressed their noses to the window and watched her.

'She's climbing the ladder!' said the clown. 'She really is!'

'She's up to the top of it!' squeaked the clockwork mouse.

'She's going right into the tree!' cried the teddy bear, and he almost broke the window with his nose, he pressed so hard against it.

Amelia Jane was climbing the tree

very well. She was a
big strong doll, and she
swung herself up easily.
She soon came to the big
thrush's nest. The mother-thrush

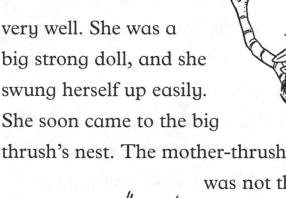

was not there.

I suppose she
has gone to
stretch her wings a
little, thought
Amelia Jane. She
stretched out her
hand and put it into
the nest. There were
four eggs there, and they
felt smooth and warm.
Amelia Jane took one and

put it into the pocket of her red dress. Then she took another, and put that in her second pocket.

'There!' she said. 'Two will be enough, I think. I can start a very nice collection with two. How pretty they are! I like them.'

She sat up in the tree for a little while, enjoying the sound of the wind in the leaves and liking the swaying of the bough she sat on. It was so exciting.

'I'd better go back now,' she said. 'I don't want to be here when the mother-thrush comes back.'

So she began to climb down the tree again. But, after a while, she

heard a noise. It was
someone whistling. She
peeped down between
the leaves.

'It's the gardener!'
said Amelia Jane
in dismay. 'Oh
dear, I hope he
isn't coming
up the tree
now.'

He wasn't. He was doing something else – something that filled Amelia Jane with great dismay.

'He's taking away the ladder! Oh my! It's gone! However am I to get down again? The ladder's gone!'

It certainly *was* gone. The gardener, still whistling, carried it away for another job. And there was Amelia Jane, left high up the tree!

She sat there for a long time. She heard the thrush come back again to her nest. She heard the wind in the trees. She saw the toys in the nursery looking out at her in surprise, wondering why she didn't climb down and come back.

'I do feel lonely and frightened,' said Amelia to herself, when the day went and the cold night began to come. 'I shall be very afraid up here in the dark. Oh dear, why ever did I think of climbing the tree and stealing eggs? It's a punishment for me, it really is!'

She began to cry. And when Amelia Jane cried she made a noise. She sobbed and gulped and howled. It was a dreadful noise.

A small pixie, who lived in the primrose bed below, heard the noise and wondered what it was. So she flew up into the tree to see.

'Oh, it's you, Amelia Jane,' said the pixie. 'What's the matter? You're keeping me awake with that dreadful noise.'

'I can't get down,' sobbed Amelia. 'I want to get back to the nursery, and I can't.'

'Whatever made you climb up?' asked the pixie. But Amelia was too ashamed to tell her.

'Please help me,' begged the big doll. 'I am so unhappy.'

'Well, maybe the thrush who lives higher up the tree can help you,' said the pixie, and she flew up to see. Amelia Jane felt most uncomfortable. She had taken eggs from the thrush's nest. Oh dear! How she wished she hadn't!

The pixie flew back again, and the
big brown thrush was with her.

'Here's the thrush,' said the pixie.
'She is very sad and unhappy tonight,
because some horrid person stole
two of her precious
eggs, but she is very
kind, and although
she is sad she
will help
you.'

'Yes, I will help you, help you, help you,' sang the thrush sweetly. 'I am sad, sad, sad, but I will help you, big, big doll.'

'How can you help me?' asked Amelia in surprise.

'I can guide you right up the tree,' said the thrush. 'I know the way. I can bring you right up to the nursery window-sill, and you can knock on the window and get the toys to let you in. Then you will be safe, safe, safe!'

'Oh, you *are* kind!' said Amelia Jane. She turned to follow the thrush up the tree.

'Hold on to one of my tail-feathers,' said the thrush kindly. 'Don't be afraid of pulling it out.'

Amelia held on to a feather, and the thrush guided her gently up the dark tree. After a little while she stopped and spoke.

'Big doll, can you see my nest just here? It is such a nice, comfortable one. It is very dark now, but perhaps you can just see two eggs gleaming in the cup. Aren't they lovely?'

Amelia Jane could see them gleaming in the half-darkness. The thrush went on, half speaking, half singing.

'You know, I had more eggs than those you see. But whilst I was away this morning someone took two, took two, took two. It nearly broke my heart. Now I shall only have two children instead of four. Can you imagine anyone bad enough to steal from a little bird like me?'

Amelia Jane felt the two eggs in her pockets, and she began to sob. 'What's the matter?' asked the kindly thrush; and she pressed her warm, feathery body close to Amelia to comfort her.

'Oh, brown thrush, oh, brown thrush,' sobbed Amelia. 'I took your eggs. I've got them in my pockets. Let me put them back into your nest, please, please! They are still lovely and warm, and I haven't broken them. I'm the horrid person that took them, but

I'm dreadfully sorry now!'

She took the warm eggs from her pockets and put them gently into the nest.

'Now push me down the tree; do anything you like to punish me!' said Amelia Jane. 'I know I deserve it.'

'What a foolish doll you are!' said the thrush, very happy to see her eggs once more. 'Because you were unkind to me is no reason why I should now be unkind to you. I am happy again, so I want to make you happy, too! Come along, hold on to my tail-feather, and we'll go higher till we come to the window-sill!'

So up they went, with Amelia wiping her eyes on her skirt every now and again because she was so ashamed of herself and so grateful to the thrush for forgiving her and being kind to her.

They came to the window-sill, and Amelia rapped on it. The teddy bear, who was just the other side, called the clown, and together they opened the window. Amelia slipped inside. She said goodbye to the thrush, and then looked at the toys.

'Whatever happened to you?' said the clown. 'Did you take the eggs? Surely that was the thrush helping you just now!'

'I did take the eggs, but I've given them back, and I'm ashamed of myself for taking them,' said Amelia in a very small voice. 'I shall never, never do such a thing again in my life. I'm going to be a Good Doll now.'

'Hmmm,' said the clown. 'We've heard that before, Amelia Jane! We'll see what the thrush has to say tomorrow!'

I heard her singing the next day, and do you know what she sang? She sang: 'Took two, took two, put them back, put them back, put them back, sweet, sweet, sweet!' Listen, and maybe you'll hear her singing that, too!

Amelia Jane and the Telephone

There was a new toy in the nursery. It was a little telephone. It stood on the nursery book-shelf looking exactly like a real one, but much smaller.

The toys didn't dare to touch it. They were afraid of the real telephone, and they were afraid of the toy one, too.

Outside in the passage they often heard the bell of the real telephone ringing loudly, and it made them jump. Then someone would come along, take the receiver off the telephone and speak into it.

'Hallo!' they would say. 'Hallo!' And then they would speak to somebody far, far away, and it all seemed very like magic.

Amelia Jane, the big naughty doll, had been away for a few days. When she came back the first thing she saw was the toy telephone.

'Aha!' she said, and went over to it. 'A telephone. Good. We need one in the nursery.'

'Don't touch it, Amelia Jane – a telephone is very magic,' cried Tom the toy soldier. 'Voices come into it, you know – people who are far, far away can speak to you. Be careful, in case somebody's voice is in that toy telephone now!'

'Pooh!' said Amelia Jane. 'I'm just going to do a bit of ordering – like Mother does sometimes on the real telephone out in the passage.'

And, to the toys' horror, she picked up the little receiver, put one end to her ear, and spoke into the other end.

'Is that the butcher? Send four sausages to the nursery, please. Is that the baker? Send four buns to the nursery, please. Is that the watchmaker? Send one nice new watch to the nursery, please – and, oh, please see that the letters A. J. are on the back. A. J. for Amelia Jane. Thank you.' She put back the receiver and smiled round at the astonished toys. 'There you are! I've done a nice little bit of ordering. We'll enjoy the sausages and the buns. We can divide them up between us. And I always wanted a watch.'

Of course, Amelia Jane knew quite well that she hadn't been speaking to the butcher, the baker and the watchmaker. She was just making the toys think she was very daring and grand.

But the toys were really very worried.
They climbed up to the window-sill to
watch for the goods to arrive.

'The thing is – how are we to pay for
them?' said the teddy bear. 'I haven't
got any money!'

'I've got a penny that I found under
the carpet,' said the clockwork mouse.

'Shall we be put into prison if we
order things we can't pay for?' asked the
clockwork clown.

Nobody knew – but they thought it
was very likely. Tom the toy soldier went
to Amelia Jane.

'Please, Amelia Jane, ring up the
butcher, the baker and the watchmaker

and tell them not to send the things after all,' he said.

'What will you give me if I do?' asked Amelia Jane at once.

'Oh dear – I'll give you my best hanky,' said Tom. 'And the mouse will give you his penny. Have *you* got anything to give, Teddy?'

'Just a good scolding,' said the teddy, rather fiercely. 'I'll give that with pleasure.'

'Give me the hanky and the money, and I'll ring up the butcher, the baker and the watchmaker,' said Amelia Jane. So they gave her them, and she went to the telephone.

'I haven't given you my scolding,'

said the bear, but Amelia took no notice. She spoke into the telephone:

'Is that the butcher? We don't want the sausages after all. Is that the baker? We don't want the buns. Is that the watchmaker? I've changed my mind about the watch. Yes – yes. That's right. What's that? You want to send a message to the teddy bear? Oh, yes, of course, I'll give it to him.'

The toys were listening with all their ears. 'Right,' said Amelia, into the telephone. 'I'm to tell the bear he is a nasty, fat, tubby little creature, who can't even growl like a bear. Yes, certainly I'll tell him!'

'Don't you dare to tell me,' said the

bear fiercely.

'All right, Teddy, I won't tell you that you are a nasty, fat, tubby little creature who can't even growl like a bear,' said Amelia Jane, annoyingly.

'But you *have* told him!' said Tom.

'No – I just told him what I wouldn't tell him,' said Amelia Jane.

She climbed up on to a shelf where nobody could reach her, not even the bear. She thought about the toy telephone. It would be very very useful, she could see that. She would be able to make up all kinds of rude messages to pass on to the toys. She began to make a little plan.

Yes – she would invent somebody at the other end – somebody who would keep ringing up – and she would pretend to answer the telephone, and then give the horrid messages to all the toys. That would keep them in order all right!

She slipped down and went to the small toy bicycle that stood at one end of the nursery. It had a tiny little bell. She unscrewed it and put it into her pocket. She could ring it whenever she wanted to – and she would pretend it was the telephone bell ringing. That would make the toys jump!

The toys made up a song about

Amelia Jane.

Amelia Jane
Is naughty again,
Let's go and leave her
Out in the rain.
Nobody loves her,
Nobody cares
If she gets eaten
By lions or bears.
She wants a scolding,
It's perfectly plain;
Amelia Jane,
You are naughty again!

Amelia listened to this song and felt very angry indeed. How dare they sing that? Why, even the clockwork mouse was singing and waving his tail about in time to the tune. Amelia walked over to the telephone and sat down by it.

She put her hand into her pocket and rang the little bell. It sounded just like the telephone bell suddenly ringing. The toys stopped singing in great surprise.

'The telephone rang!' they said to one another. 'Would you believe it? The telephone rang. Answer it, Amelia. See who wants to speak to us.'

Amelia picked up the receiver and put one end to her ear. 'Dear me – is that really Mr Mumbo-Jumbo?' she said, sounding astonished. 'This is Amelia Jane. What do you want, dear Mr Mumbo-Jumbo?'

The toys listened to this in

amazement. Amelia Jane went on speaking. 'Yes, yes – I'll tell the bear. You're coming for him this evening, and you'll pull his nose for him till it's as long as an elephant's trunk. Yes, Mr Mumbo-Jumbo. Oh, yes – he is a bad bear. He deserves it. I'm sorry he was once so rude to you. Goodbye.'

She put down the receiver. The bear was trembling like a jelly, he was so scared.

'I was never rude to Mr Mumbo-Jumbo,' he wailed. 'I don't even know him. I never met him. I won't have my nose pulled, I won't, I won't.'

'I won't let you,' said Tom, comfortingly. 'I'll fight him.'

'So will I,' said the clockwork mouse, bravely. 'I'll nibble a hole in his leg.'

The telephone bell rang again – though, of course, it was only Amelia Jane putting her hand into her pocket and ringing the little bicycle bell. She picked up the receiver again and spoke into it.

'Hallo! Who's that? Oh, Mr Mumbo-Jumbo again – what do you want this time, dear Mr Mumbo-Jumbo? Yes, the clockwork mouse lives here – and the toy soldier too. No, they are not very nice toys. What am I to tell them? You are coming tonight to catch the toy soldier and peg him to your clothes-line? And you're going to peg the clockwork mouse up by his tail? Right, I'll tell them. Goodbye.'

'Oooooh!' squealed the clockwork mouse in fright. 'He's not to come! I never did him any harm!'

'Nor did I,' said Tom, turning pale. 'Who's this awful fellow? He's not to come. I've never been pegged up on a clothes-line in my life, and nobody's going to do that to me.'

The bell rang again and Amelia Jane once more spoke into the telephone. 'Oh – it's you, Mr Mumbo-Jumbo, again. What's that? You'll scold any toy who is rude to me? Thank you very much indeed. I'll tell you tonight who you can scold very severely!'

She made a rude face at the listening toys and went over to her cot. She climbed in. 'I'm going to have a good sleep,' she said. 'And anyone who disturbs me will be reported to Mr Mumbo-Jumbo!'

She shut her eyes and was soon fast asleep. She turned in her sleep – and out of her pocket fell the little bicycle bell!

The clockwork clown pounced on it.

'Look at that! She rang this when she wanted us to think it was the telephone ringing! It was all a pretence on her part, the wicked doll. There wasn't any Mr Mumbo-Jumbo speaking to her over the telephone!'

'Let's wake her,' said Tom fiercely.

'No,' said the clown, speaking in a whisper. 'I've got a better idea. I know where there's a long piece of rubber tubing. I'll get it and fix it to the ear-piece of the telephone – and then, whoever speaks at the other end of the rubber tube can be heard in the telephone – *really* heard, not just pretending.'

'What's the use of that?' asked the bear.

'Wait and see,' said the clown. 'Now tonight one of us will ring this little bell, as if the telephone was ringing again – and Amelia can go and answer it – and Tom shall speak through the tube . . .'

'Oooooh, yes,' said everyone. 'That's a fine idea!'

'And he shall say, in a very dreadful voice: "This is Mr Mumbo-Jumbo speaking. Is that Amelia Jane? I've heard what a bad doll you are. And I'm coming to get you, Amelia. I'm walking up the passage now – I'm banging at the door. Let me in!"'

'But – what's the good of that?' said

the bear. 'He won't come walking up and banging at the door.'

'Yes, he will,' grinned the clown. 'I shall be outside, listening – and *I'll* come stamping up the passage, and *I'll* bang hard at the door – see?'

'Amelia will think it's really Mr Mumbo-Jumbo out there and she'll be scared out of her life!' said the bear, chuckling. 'What a fine idea. Where's the rubber tube, clown?'

Well, before Amelia woke up, the rubber tubing was fixed to the telephone and run secretly into the toy-cupboard, where Tom was hiding. They all waited till Amelia awoke and stepped out of the cot.

At the same moment the bear, who was by the telephone, rang the little bell that had fallen from Amelia's pocket. 'R-r-r-r-ring!'

Amelia jumped and looked surprised. But she walked over to the telephone and took off the receiver, meaning to make up some more messages from Mumbo-Jumbo. But to her astonishment and horror, a deep, hollow voice came to her ear.

'Is that Amelia Jane? This is Mr Mumbo-Jumbo speaking. I've heard what a bad doll you are. And I'm coming to get you, Amelia. I'm walking up the passage now – I'm BANGING at the door. Let me in!'

Amelia listened in fright. There really was somebody speaking through the telephone this time – somebody who said he was *Mr Mumbo-Jumbo*!

Then she heard the footsteps stamping up the passage outside, where the clown had hidden himself. She heard the loud banging at the door, and the shouts of 'Let me in!'

'No, no – don't let him in!' she wailed, and she ran to the toy- cupboard. 'Don't open the door, toys. I'll be good. I'll never be bad again. I'll give you back your hanky, Tom, and your money, Mouse. Oh, oh, don't let Mr Mumbo-Jumbo in.'

Bang-bang-BANG! 'Let me in, I say!'

Amelia piled bricks all over herself in the cupboard, trying to hide. Tom went to the door of the nursery and spoke sternly through it.

'Go away, Mr Mumbo-Jumbo. We will let you know if Amelia Jane is

naughty again, and you can come and get her then.'

And to Amelia's great relief she heard footsteps stamping away from the door, and the banging stopped.

'Well, we've saved you from your friend, Mr Mumbo-Jumbo,' said Tom, looking into the cupboard. 'Are you going to behave yourself now, or not?'

'Oh, yes, yes,' sobbed Amelia Jane. 'Oh, that awful toy telephone. I'll never use it again.'

She didn't, of course. And, strange to say, neither did Mr Mumbo-Jumbo!

Now Then, Amelia Jane!

Amelia Jane, the big naughty doll in the nursery, was doing a bit of sewing. She sat in the corner, her head bent over her work, sewing away.

'Aha! So you've decided to sew on that shoe button at last!' said the clockwork clown, coming up. 'Quite time, too – your shoe's fallen off heaps of times!'

'You be quiet,' said Amelia Jane.

'And while you're about it, why not mend that hole in your dress?' said a wooden skittle, hopping up. 'Or do you *like* holes in your dress, Amelia Jane?'

'You be quiet, too,' said Amelia, and

jabbed at him with her needle. He hopped away with a chuckle.

He was soon back again. 'And what about your right stocking?' he said. 'It's got a great big hole in the heel. And what about . . . ?'

Amelia Jane jabbed at him again so hard that the thimble flew off her finger. It rolled away over the floor into a corner.

'Bother you, skittle!' said Amelia Jane, in a temper. 'Now you go and pick up that thimble and bring it back to me! Why do you tease me like this? I don't like you.'

'Shan't pick up your thimble!' said the skittle, enjoying himself. 'Silly old

Amelia Jane!'

'Stop yelling at one another, and you go and pick up the thimble, skittle,' said the teddy bear, crossly. 'Can't you see I'm trying to read?'

The skittle didn't dare to disobey the big fat bear. He had once been rude to the bear and the bear had sat on him for a whole day, and the skittle hadn't liked that at all. The bear was so heavy.

So he picked up the thimble – but he didn't give it back to Amelia Jane. No – he put it on his head for a hat!

Then he walked up and down in a very silly way, saying, 'Look at my new hat! Oh, *do* look at my new hat!'

Everybody looked, of course, and all the toys laughed at the skittle because he really did look funny
in a thimble-hat.

He took it off and bowed to them, and then put it back again.

'*Will* you give me my thimble?' cried Amelia Jane, in a rage. 'Give it to me AT ONCE!'

'Say "please", Amelia,' said the bear. 'You sound very rude.'

'I *shan't* say "please"!' cried Amelia. 'And don't you interfere. Skittle, if you don't give me back my thimble at once

I'll chase you and knock you over!'

'Can't catch me! Can't catch me!' said the skittle, who was really being very funny and very annoying. He ran here and there, and he kept taking his thimble-hat on and off to Amelia in a very ridiculous way.

Well, Amelia Jane wasn't going to let a skittle be cheeky to her, so up she got.

She raced after the skittle, and he rushed away. But Amelia Jane caught him – and do you know what she did? Instead of taking the thimble off his head, she pushed it so hard that it went right over the poor skittle's nose, and he couldn't see a thing.

'Oh! Oh, it's so tight now I can't get it off!' yelled the skittle, trying to force the thimble off his head.

Amelia Jane laughed.

'That'll teach you to wear my thimble for a hat and be so rude to me,' she said.

'Help, help!' shouted the skittle. 'It's hurting me! Ooooooooooh! Ow! OOOOOOOOOOOH!'

'It really is hurting him,' said the bear, getting up. 'Dear, dear – I shall never finish my book today. Stand still, you silly skittle. I'll take the thimble off.'

Well, he tugged and he pulled, and he pulled and he tugged – but he couldn't get that thimble off!

Then Tom the toy soldier came up and had a try – but he couldn't get the thimble off either.

Amelia Jane tried – but it wasn't a bit of good; that thimble was jammed so hard on the skittle's head that it really could *not* be moved!

'You'll have to wear the thimble always,' said the bear at last. The skittle lay down and yelled.

'I can't! I don't want to! Take it off, take it off! It's tight, I tell you!'

'We'll simply *have* to do something,' said Tom. 'Else the skittle will go on yelling for ever, and I don't think I could bear that.'

'Of *course* something must be done,' said the other skittles, who had popped up, looking very worried. 'Amelia Jane is very naughty.'

'That's nothing new,' said the bear. 'Dear me, do stop yelling, skittle. You'll wake up the household!'

Then the bear thought of something. 'Oh, I've got an idea,' he said. 'What about going out to ask the little pixie who lives in the pansy bed if he knows of a spell to help us. A Get-Loose Spell, perhaps.'

'A good idea,' said Tom. 'Amelia Jane, go and find the pixie and ask him.'

'What! In the middle of a dark night!' said Amelia Jane. 'No, thank you. And anyway, I don't like that pixie!'

'Amelia Jane, if you don't go and ask him, we shall take your best ribbon and hide it,' said the bear.

'Oh, no, don't do that!' said Amelia. 'It's my party ribbon. All right, you horrid things – I'll go. But I know a very good way of getting the thimble off the skittle.'

'How?' asked the toys.

'Chop off his head!' said Amelia Jane. 'He has so few brains that he'd never even notice his head was gone!'

'We *will* take away your best ribbon now,' said the bear, as the skittle gave a loud yell of fright.

'No, no – I didn't mean it!' said Amelia Jane. 'I'll go this very minute to find the pixie.'

Well, off she went, climbing out of the window and down to the pansy bed.

The little pixie was there, wide awake.

'Pixie,' began Amelia, 'I want your help.'

'What will you give me for it?' asked the pixie, at once. He didn't like Amelia.

'Nothing,' said Amelia. 'Oh – let go of my foot, you horrid little pixie!'

'I'm taking your shoe for payment,' said the pixie. 'And the other one too. They will fit me nicely. Now, it's no good yelling. I've got them. I've no doubt you've been just as naughty as usual, so it serves you right. Now – what do you want my help for?'

Amelia Jane told him sulkily. 'The skittle is wearing my thimble jammed down hard on his head. How can we get it off?'

'Make the thimble bigger, of course,' said the pixie. 'Then his head will be too small for it and it will slip off.'

'But how can we make the thimble

bigger?' asked Amelia Jane.

'Easy,' said the pixie. 'If you heat anything made of metal it becomes just a tiny bit larger – so heat the thimble, Amelia – and it will slip off the skittle's head.'

'But how can we heat it?' said Amelia, not really believing the pixie.

'Stand him on his head in hot water,' said the pixie. 'You could have thought of that yourself. Now go away. I want to try on your shoes.'

Amelia went back to the nursery. 'The pixie says that if we stand the skittle on his head in hot water, the thimble will get a bit larger and slip off,' said Amelia.

'I don't believe a word of it,' said the bear.

'Well, that's what he *said*,' said Amelia. 'He didn't tell me anything else. And I had to give him my shoes for that advice.'

'Hm,' said Tom. 'Well, poor old skittle – we'd better try it, anyway. Bear, put a little hot water into the basin, will you? Don't put the plug in in case it gets too deep – just let the water run in and out, and we'll pop the skittle in on his head, and heat the thimble in the water.'

Well, the skittle howled and yelled and kicked up a great fuss, but the bear and the toy soldier were very firm with him. They turned him upside down and held him in the hot water, so that the heat warmed up the thimble on his head.

And will you believe it? – the thimble slipped off, just as the pixie had said it would. But alas – it rolled round the basin, and disappeared down the plughole! It was gone!

'Oh – my thimble, my thimble!' yelled Amelia Jane. But it was gone for good. Nobody ever saw it again.

'Serves you right, Amelia,' said the bear, turning the poor skittle the right way up again.

'Well,

who would have thought the pixie knew a spell like that? Did *you* know that heat made things just a bit bigger, clockwork clown?'

'I never did,' said the clown.

But the funny thing is that it's *true*! So if ever a thimble gets stuck on one of your skittles you'll know what to do – stand him on his head in hot water and it will slip off!

And now Amelia Jane can't *bear* doing her mending, because she hasn't got a thimble and she pricks her finger all the time. Still, as the toys tell her – it's her own fault!

Amelia Jane Gets Into Trouble

Amelia Jane, as you all know, is a very clever and very naughty doll. The toys could never keep pace with her tricks – but one day she got herself into trouble.

It happened like this. Billy came into the nursery and looked round for his soldier doll. 'Tom, where are you?' he said. 'I'm going to take you to tea with me this afternoon and I'm going in *my* soldier things, too! We're going to play with Betty and Dick, and they're going to dress up as soldiers as well. So, with you, we'll be four soldiers! We'll have fun!'

He began looking for Tom, the soldier. But before he could find him his mother called out. 'Billy! Come here a minute. I want you.'

Billy ran out. Amelia Jane sat up, her eyes gleaming. 'Tom, don't you go! They'll do awful things to you!'

'Oh dear!'

said Tom, in alarm. Although he was a soldier doll, he wasn't at all brave really. 'Oh dear! I don't want to go. I really don't!'

'Well, I'll go instead,' said Amelia Jane, in a kind voice. 'I'll do you a good turn and put on your clothes and go instead of you. Would you like that?'

'Oh, yes!' said Tom. He stripped off his soldier clothes, and Amelia Jane dressed herself up in them. My word, she did look different. You should have seen her! She pranced about looking very smart in Tom's trousers and jacket. 'I'm grand! I'm brave!'

She began to rush at the toys, pretending to capture them. They didn't like it at all.

'Now stop that, Amelia Jane!' said the sailor doll. 'And take off those clothes. You know perfectly well that nobody will harm Tom if he goes out to tea – you've only said that because you want to dress up and prance about pretending to be a soldier. Take those clothes off.'

But all that Amelia Jane did was to rush at the toy clown and the sailor doll, and pretend to capture them. They were very cross indeed – but Amelia was bigger than they were, and it was difficult to stop her.

In rushed Billy. He caught hold of Amelia Jane, thinking she was Tom, his soldier doll. Out of the door he went at top speed, calling out, 'I'm ready, Mother! I'm just coming!'

Amelia Jane planned to have a wonderful time. She would go stalking Betty and Dick with Billy. She would take them prisoner. My goodness, Amelia Jane was going to have the time of her life!

But it didn't turn out quite like that. Billy, Betty and Dick got the gardener to hide Amelia Jane somewhere, so that they could stalk her and pounce on her and take her prisoner!

So Amelia was put into the middle of a bush by the gardener, and left there. The children began to hunt for her, going along in single file, leaping high in the air, and filling the garden with loud cries.

Amelia Jane shivered in the bush. How she hoped they wouldn't find her. She didn't mind stalking the others and pouncing on them – but she didn't want to be pounced on and taken prisoner herself!

Well, the children soon found her. They surrounded the bush, and Betty yelled out loudly: 'The enemy is hiding here! I see him! Come on, soldiers, come on!'

And they all pounced! Amelia Jane was pulled roughly from the bush and thrown to the ground.

'You're our prisoner!' yelled the three, and ran round her. They didn't even touch Amelia, but she thought they were going to every time they came.

'Let's tie him to a tree,' said Billy. So they took Amelia and tied her to a little tree.

'Funny sort of doll, this,' said Dick, looking closely at her. 'He's got a face

more like a girl-doll than a boy-doll.'

'Now he's tied up. He can't get away. He's our prisoner,' said Betty.

But fortunately for Amelia Jane, the tea-bell rang loudly, and the three soldiers raced up to the house in glee.

Amelia Jane began to sob. She

struggled with the knots that tied her, but they were tight and she couldn't undo even one of them. She was very frightened. How she wished she hadn't been silly enough to make Tom give her his clothes!

'I'm always doing silly things!' wept Amelia. 'I wish I didn't. Oh, what shall I do?'

She waited for the children to come back. She waited and she waited. But they didn't come. Betty's mother had said she thought it was going to rain, so they could either play a *quiet* game of soldiers indoors, or a noisy game of snap, whichever they liked.

They chose snap, and forgot all

about Amelia Jane, tied to the tree in the garden. In fact Billy forgot about her completely, and even went home without her! So there she was when darkness came, still tied up tightly, jumping in fright every time an owl came by and hooted.

The toys were surprised when Billy came home without Amelia Jane. He didn't say anything about leaving her behind until just before he went to bed. He was sitting in his pyjamas eating his supper in the nursery with his sister, when he suddenly gave a cry.

'What's the matter?' said his mother.

'It's Tom. I've forgotten to bring him home,' said Billy. 'We tied him up to a tree and then we went in to tea and I forgot all about him. He's still there, poor thing. And it's dark and rainy. Mother, I must go and get him.'

'No, you mustn't,' said his mother, firmly. 'You are certainly not going to run down the dark rainy street in your pyjamas. You can get Tom tomorrow. If he's under a tree he won't get very wet.'

'But he'll be frightened,' said Billy. 'He won't like it.'

'Well, that's your fault,' said his mother. 'When we forget things we often make others suffer as well as ourselves. You should have remembered to bring Tom home.'

Now, of course, the toys couldn't

help hearing all this, because they were sitting round the nursery watching the children eat their supper. They were full of horror.

What! Amelia Jane tied up to a tree, left alone in the darkness and the rain! Naughty as she was, and cross as they felt with her, they were very sorry. When the children had gone to bed they got together in a corner and talked about it.

'I'll go and rescue her,' said Tom, bravely. 'I know the way. I've been to that house before.'

'But you haven't got any clothes on,' said the sailor doll. 'You'll get soaked. And it's frightening to go out in the dark at night. You might meet a fierce dog or a yowling cat who would pounce on you. Anyway, you're not very brave.'

'Oh, I know that,' said Tom, sadly. 'It's a pity to have to be a soldier doll and not feel brave. That's really why I'm going. I'm not brave, in fact I'm very frightened, but I feel I *ought* to be brave, so I'm going to rescue Amelia.'

'Well, that's very nice of you, after she tricked you into taking off your clothes and letting her go out to tea instead of you,' said the toy clown, patting Tom on the back. 'All right, you go then, if you know the way. What about clothes? There's a little cape and hat in the doll's wardrobe. You could borrow those.'

So Tom put them on and he looked rather odd, not at all like a soldier doll! Then he slipped out of the window, climbed down the tree outside and set off in the darkness to Betty's house.

The rain hit him on the nose, and ran down his cloak in little rivers. It went down his neck too, because his hat didn't fit very well. At last he came to the garden of Betty's house and slipped through a hole in the fence.

Amelia Jane was still tied to the tree. An owl had hooted in her ear. A spider had walked over her face. A hedgehog had walked so near that his spines pricked her legs. She was lonely and scared.

She heard a noise. What was that? Oh, what was that? It sounded like someone coming nearer and nearer, creeping through the bushes! Amelia began to tremble and shake.

'Who is it? Go away! Leave me alone! Oh, don't come near me, I'm scared, I'm frightened! Don't frighten me any more. Go away, whoever it is!'

But the footsteps came nearer and nearer, and then a head poked round a bush. Amelia Jane gave a scream.

'Go away! I'm frightened of you!'

Well it was Tom, of course, come to rescue her! 'It's all right,' he said. 'It's only me, Tom. I'll undo your knots, Amelia Jane.'

Amelia could have hugged him! Dear, dear Tom! Oh, how could she have tricked him like that! She would always, always love him now.

He undid the knots. She stretched herself stiffly and then sneezed. 'Let's hurry home,' said Tom. 'You've caught a cold. I'll lead the way.'

Well, it wasn't long before they were both back in the nursery again, leaving little wet marks all over the

floor. As soon as they got there Amelia Jane flung herself on Tom and hugged him so hard that he squealed.

'Good, kind, *brave* Tom! Oh, what courage you've got! Oh, how plucky you are! Toys, Tom is quite the bravest toy in the nursery!'

Tom could hardly believe his ears when all the toys crowded round and thumped him on the back, and said the same as Amelia! 'But I'm not brave!' he kept saying. 'I never have been! I was frightened all the time. Brave people aren't frightened.'

'The bravest people of all are those who are frightened and yet go on being brave,' said the sailor doll, helping him off with his wet cloak. 'Amelia Jane has no right to wear a soldier's clothes – she's a little coward! As soon as they are dry, you must wear them again, because you really and truly are a brave soldier!'

The toys dried Tom's clothes, as soon as Amelia Jane had taken them off. Amelia dressed humbly in her own clothes. She felt ashamed of herself. She sneezed loudly.

'I'm getting a dreadful cold,' she said, very sorry for herself.

'It serves you right,' said the sailor doll. 'Don't sneeze all over us, please. We're giving a party for Tom soon, and you'd better not come in case you give everyone your cold.'

So now Amelia Jane is sitting by herself in a corner sneezing into her hanky, watching the most wonderful party going on, given for Tom, the soldier doll. Nobody feels at all sorry for her. I don't know if you do?

Billy's going to be very surprised tomorrow to find that Tom is sitting in the nursery instead of tied up to the tree! He's going to puzzle about that for days.

Amelia Jane Has a Good Idea

The new teddy bear was very small indeed. The toys stared at him when he first came into the playroom, wondering what he was.

'Good gracious! I believe you're a teddy bear!' said Amelia Jane, the big, naughty doll. 'I thought you were a peculiar-shaped mouse.'

'Well, I'm not,' said the small bear,

sharply, and pressed himself in the middle. 'Grrrrrr! Hear me growl? Well, no mouse can growl. It can only squeak.'

GGGRRR!

'Yes. You're a bear all right,' said Tom, coming up. 'I hear you've come to live with us. Well, I'll show you your place in the toy-cupboard – right at the back there, look.'

'I don't like being at the back, it's too dark,' said the little bear. 'I'll be at the front here, by this big brick-box.'

'Oh, no you won't. That's *my* place when I want to sit in the toy-cupboard,' said Amelia Jane. 'And let me tell you this, small bear – if you live with us you'll have to take on lots of little bits of work. We all do. You'll have to wind up the clockwork clown when he runs down, you'll have to clean the dolls'-house windows, and you'll have to help the engine-driver polish his big red train.'

'Dear me, I don't think I want to do any of those things,' said the bear. 'I'm lazy. I don't like working.'

'Well, you'll just have to,' said Amelia Jane. 'Otherwise you won't get any of the biscuit crumbs that the children drop on the floor, you won't get any of the sweets in the toy sweet-shop – and we're allowed some every week –

and you won't come to any parties. So there.'

'Pooh!' said the bear and stalked off to pick up some beads out of the bead-box and thread himself a necklace.

'He's vain as well as lazy,' said Tom in disgust. 'Hey, bear – what's your name? Or are you too lazy to have one?'

'My name is Sidney Gordon Eustace,' said the bear, haughtily. 'And please remember that I don't like being called Sid.'

'Sid!' yelled all the toys at once, and the bear looked furious. He turned his head away, and went on threading the beads.

'Sidney Gordon Eustace!' said the

clown, with a laugh. 'I guess he gave himself those names. No sensible child would ever call a teddy bear that. Huh!'

The bear was not much use in the playroom. He just would *not* do any of the jobs there at all. He went surprisingly deaf when anyone called to him to come and clean or polish or sweep. He would pretend to be asleep, or just walk about humming a little tune as if nobody was calling his name at all. It was most annoying.

'Sidney! Come and shake the mats for the dolls'-house dolls!' Tom called. No answer from Sidney at all. 'SIDNEY! Come here! You're not as deaf as all that!'

The bear never even turned his head.

'Hey, Sidney Gordon Eustace – come and do your jobs!' yelled Tom. 'SID, SID, SID!'

No answer. 'All right!' shouted Tom, angrily. 'You shan't have that nice big crumb of chocolate biscuit we found under the table this morning.'

It was always the same whenever there was a job to be done. 'Sidney, come here!' But Sidney never came. He never did one single thing for any of the toys.

'What are we going to do about him?' said the big teddy bear. 'Amelia Jane – can't you think of a good idea?'

'Oh, yes,' said Amelia at once. 'I

know what we'll do. We'll get Sidney-the-mouse to come and do the things that Sidney-the-bear should do – and he shall have all the crumbs and titbits that the bear should have. He won't like that – a little house-mouse getting all his treats!'

'Dear me – is the house-mouse's name Sidney, too?' said Tom in surprise. 'I never knew that before. When we want him we usually go to his hole and shout "Mouse" and he comes.'

'Well, I'll go and shout "Sidney",' said Amelia Jane, 'and you'll see – he'll come!' So she went to the little hole at the bottom of the wall near the bookcase and shouted down it.

'Sidney! Sid-Sid-Sidney! We want you!'

The little bear, of course, didn't turn round – *he* wasn't going to come when his name was called. But someone very small came scampering up the passage to the hole-entrance. It was the tiny brown house-mouse, with bright black eyes and twitching whiskers.

'Ah, Sidney,' said Amelia Jane. 'Will you just come and shake the mats in the dolls' house, please? They are very dusty. We'll give you a big chocolate biscuit crumb and a drink of lemonade out of the little teapot if you will.'

'Can I drink out of the spout?' said the tiny mouse, pleased. 'I like drinking

out of the spout.'

'Yes, of course,' said Amelia Jane.

The little mouse set about shaking the mats vigorously, and the job was soon done.

'Isn't Sidney wonderful?' said Amelia in a loud voice to the others. 'Sidney-the-mouse, I mean, of course, not silly Sidney-the-bear. He wouldn't have the strength to shake mats like that, poor thing. Sidney, here's the chocolate biscuit crumb and there's the teapot full of lemonade.'

Sidney the bear didn't like this at all. Fancy making a fuss of a silly little mouse, and giving him treats like that. He would very much have liked the crumb and the lemonade himself. He pressed himself in the middle and growled furiously when the mouse had gone.

'Don't have that mouse here again,' he said. 'I don't like hearing somebody else being called Sidney. Anyway, I don't believe his name *is* Sidney. It's not a name for a mouse.'

'Well, for all you know, his name might be Sidney Gordon Eustace just like yours,' said Amelia Jane at once.

'Pooh! Whoever heard of a mouse

having a grand name like that?' said the bear.

'Well, next time you won't do a job, we'll call all three names down the hole,' said Amelia, 'and see if the little mouse will answer to them!'

Next night there was going to be a party. Everyone had to help to get ready for it. Amelia Jane called to the little bear.

'Sidney! Come and set the tables for the party. Sidney, do you hear me?'

Sidney did, but he pretended not to, of course. Set party tables! Not he! So he went deaf again, and didn't even turn his head.

'Sidney Gordon Eustace, do as

you're told or you won't come to the party,' bawled the big teddy bear in a fine old rage.

The little bear didn't answer. Amelia Jane gave a sudden grin.

'Never mind,' she said. 'We'll get Sidney Gordon Eustace, the little mouse, to come and set the tables. He does them beautifully and never breaks a thing. He can come to the party afterwards then. I'll call him.'

The little bear turned his head. 'He won't answer to *that* name, you know he won't!' he said, scornfully. 'Call away! No mouse ever had a name as grand as mine.'

Amelia Jane went to the mouse-hole

and called down it.

'Sidney Gordon Eustace, are you there?' she called. 'If you are at home, come up and help us. Sidney Gordon Eustace, are you there?'

And at once there came the pattering of tiny feet, and with a loud squeak the little mouse peeped out of his hole, his whiskers quivering.

'Ah – you are at home,' said Amelia. 'Well, dear little Sidney, will you set the tables for us? We're going to have a party.'

The mouse was delighted. He was soon at work, and in a short while the four tables were set with tiny table-cloths and china. Then he went to help the dolls'-house dolls to cut sandwiches. The bear watched all this out of the corner of his eye. He was quite amazed that the mouse had come when he was called Sidney Gordon Eustace – goodness, fancy a little mouse owning a name like that!

He was very cross when he saw that the mouse was going to the party. Amelia Jane found him a red ribbon to tie round his neck and one for his long tail. He was given a place at the biggest table, and everyone made a fuss of him.

'Good little Sidney! You do work well! Whatever should we do without you? What will you have to eat?'

The mouse ate a lot. *Much* too much, the little bear thought. He didn't go to the party. He hadn't been asked and he didn't quite like to go because there was no chair for him and no plate. But, oh, all those nice things to eat! *Why* hadn't he been sensible and gone to set the tables?

'Goodnight, Sidney Gordon Eustace,' said Amelia to the delighted mouse. 'We've loved having you.'

Now, after this kind of thing had happened three or four times the bear got tired of it.

He hated hearing people yell for 'Sidney, Sidney!' down the mouse-hole, or to hear the mouse addressed as Sidney Gordon Eustace. It was really too bad. Also, the mouse was getting all the titbits and the treats. The bear didn't like that either.

So the next time that there was a job to be done the bear decided to do it. He suddenly heard Tom say 'Hallo! The big red engine is very smeary. It wants a polish again. I'll go and call Sidney.'

Tom went to the mouse-hole and began to call down it. 'Sidney, Sidney, Sidney!'

But before the mouse could answer, Sidney the bear rushed up to Tom. 'Yes!

Did you call me? What do you want me to do?'

'Dear me – you're not as deaf as usual!' said Tom, surprised. 'Well, go and polish the red engine, then. You can have a sweet out of the toy sweet shop if you do it properly.'

Sidney did do it properly. Tom came and looked at the engine and so did Amelia Jane. 'Very nice,' said Amelia. 'Give him a big sweet, Tom.'

The bear was pleased. Aha! He had done the mouse out of a job. The toys had been pleased with him, and the sweet was delicious.

And after that, dear me, you should have seen Sidney the bear rush up

whenever
his name was
called. 'Yes, yes – here I am.
What do you want me to do?'

Very soon the little mouse was not
called up from the hole any more, and
Sidney the bear worked hard and was
friendly and sensible. The toys began to
like him, and Sidney liked them too.

But one thing puzzled Tom and the
big teddy bear, and they asked Amelia
Jane about it.

'Amelia Jane – HOW did you know that the mouse's name was Sidney Gordon Eustace?'

'It isn't,' said Amelia with a grin.

'But it must be,' said Tom. 'He always came when you called him by it.'

'I know – but he'd come if you called *any* name down his hole,' said Amelia. 'Go and call what name you like – he'll come! It's the calling he answers, not the name! He doesn't even know what names are!'

'Good gracious!' said Tom and the bear, and they went to the mouse-hole.

'William!' called Tom, and up came the mouse. He was given a crumb and went down again.

'Polly-Wolly-Doodle!' shouted the big bear, and up came the mouse for another crumb.

'Boot-polish!' shouted Tom, and up came the mouse.

'Tomato soup!' cried the big bear.

And it didn't matter what name was yelled down the hole, the mouse always came up. He came because he heard a loud shout, that was all. Amelia Jane went off into fits of laughter when the mouse came up at different calls. 'Penny stamp! Cough-drop! Sid-Sid-Sid! Dickory-Dock! Rub-a-dub-dub!'

The mouse's nose appeared at the hole each time. How the toys laughed – all except Sidney the bear!

He didn't laugh. He felt very silly indeed. Oh, dear – what a trick Amelia Jane had played on him! But suddenly he began to laugh, too. 'It's funny,' he cried. 'It's funny!'

It certainly was. Amelia *would* think of a good idea like that, wouldn't she?

Amelia Jane is Very Busy

One day Amelia Jane sat very still in her little chair, and watched somebody knitting in the playroom. It was little Miss Jones, who came to help with the children's clothes. She was knitting a jersey for the biggest boy.

'Click-click-clickety-click!' Her knitting needles flashed in and out all day long, and Amelia Jane watched and watched.

When little Miss Jones had finished
all the knitting and had put the balls of
left-over wool neatly in the work-basket
with the long needles, she left the
playroom to go home.

As soon as she had gone Amelia Jane
ran to the work-basket. She took up two
needles and a ball of wool and went to
sit on the rug by herself, leaning
against the table-leg.

'I can knit,' she
told the toys. 'I
know how
to. I watched
Miss Jones
all day

long. You go like this – and like that – and see, the knitting comes!'

The toys watched her. They thought Amelia Jane was very clever. Click-click-clickity-click – why, her needles went as fast as Miss Jones' needles!

'What are you making?' asked the sailor doll.

'Nothing. I'm just knitting,' said Amelia.

'But you must be knitting *something*,' said the clockwork mouse. 'You can't just *knit*.'

'It's a waste of wool not to make something when you knit,' said the teddy bear. 'Can't you make me a jersey?'

'No. It would take me ages to knit a jersey to go over your fat little tummy,' said Amelia Jane.

'Don't be rude,' said the bear, offended. 'If *you* kept a growl in your tummy, you'd be fat, too. Grrr!'

'Couldn't you knit me a bonnet?' said the baby doll. 'I could do with a new one.'

'No, I couldn't. You've got three already,' said Amelia Jane. 'For goodness' sake go away and let me *knit*! I tell you, I'm not making anything at all, I'm just knitting.'

The baby doll sat down by her and took off her hair-ribbon to smooth it out. She was very particular about her ribbons. She put it down beside her, and began to comb out her hair with a little comb.

'Go away,' said Amelia. 'I don't like people who comb hair all over me.'

'Well, you can just put up with it,' said the baby doll, crossly. 'I can sit where I like.'

Amelia Jane didn't say anything – but when the baby doll looked for her hair-ribbon it had gone!

'You've taken it!' she said to Amelia. 'You mean thing. Give it back.'

'She can't. She's knitted it with the wool!' said Tom, pointing. And sure enough that bad Amelia Jane had taken the ribbon and knitted it – and there was the ribbon, right in the very middle of the knitting.

'I can't take it out,' said Amelia. 'It would spoil my beautiful knitting. You'll have to do without your ribbon now. It's your own fault.'

The baby doll went off, crying. 'Cry-baby!' said Amelia Jane, and went on knitting.

'Your knitting is nothing but a long, long scarf, very narrow,' said the bear. 'It's silly knitting. Nobody would wear a scarf like that.'

'Nobody's going to,' said Amelia Jane. 'I wish you would stop bothering me. Can't I knit if I want to?'

'The click-click noise makes me

cross,' said the sailor doll.

'It doesn't take much to make you cross,' said Amelia. 'Clockwork mouse, what do *you* want? Don't you dare to nibble my wool!'

'I just want to watch you knit,' said the mouse, and he sat down close by. And will you believe it, that rascally Amelia Jane knitted his long tail into her knitting! The little mouse suddenly

found himself pulled towards Amelia's knitting, and saw his tail there!

Goodness, what a to-do there was! The bear was very angry. 'You can't do things like this, Amelia!' he said.

'I can,' she said. 'And I have. The mouse can't have his tail back. It belongs to my knitting now.'

But the sailor doll made her undo the tail because the clockwork mouse was so upset.

'He can't hang on to your knitting by his tail,' he told Amelia Jane.

'You're very unkind and very silly. Just *look* at the enormous length of knitting you have done – all for nothing, too!'

The next thing he knew was that Amelia had pulled out his bootlaces and had knitted those, too! She would not give them back, either, and the sailor doll stamped round the nursery in a rage, his boots slipping off his feet every minute!

'She'll have to fall asleep sometime soon,' whispered the teddy bear to the toy soldier. 'Then we'll pay her out for all this!'

So they waited till her needles worked more and more slowly – clickity-click, clickity-click – click – click – click – click – and then they stopped. Amelia Jane was fast asleep!

The toys crept up to her. They took

up the long, long strip of knitting. They wound it all round Amelia Jane and the table-leg she was leaning against – round and round and round and round!

'Now she's all tied up in her own knitting!' said Tom, pleased. 'And the more she knits, the more tied up she will get.'

Amelia Jane woke up merry and bright. She picked up her knitting

needles and started off again – clickity-click, clickity-click!

But soon she found that she was bound tightly to the table-leg, and the more she pulled at her knitting, the tighter it became. She tried to stand up – but she couldn't.

'Oh! Oh! I've knitted myself to the table-leg!' she cried. 'Toys, help me!'

'Certainly *not*,' said the clockwork clown with a squeal of delight. 'Go on knitting. You'll soon be right in the middle of it and we shan't see you again! Knit hard, Amelia, knit hard!'

Amelia Jane didn't. She stopped. She tugged at the knitting to try to free herself but she couldn't. And dear me, how scared she got when she saw how the knitting was wound round and round and round herself and the table-leg!

'Undo me!' she begged the baby doll.

'I will if you knit me a new bonnet,' said the doll.

'Undo me!' Amelia Jane begged the bear.

'I will if you knit me a jersey and don't say anything about my fat little tummy,' said the bear.

'And you can knit me a red waistcoat,' said Tom.

'And me a new vest,' said the sailor doll.

'All right,' said Amelia. 'You're

mean, all of you. But I'll knit what you want – and I hope nothing fits, so there!'

Well, they undid Amelia Jane from the table-leg, and then they helped her to pull undone all the long, long piece of knitting.

Out came the sailor's bootlaces and the baby doll's ribbon!

And then she had to set to work to keep her promises. She has made the bear a tight little red jersey.

'You'll never be able to get it off again, once you've got it on,' Tom told him, so the poor bear can't make up his mind whether to wear it or not.

Amelia has made the sailor a new vest, but as it reaches down to his feet he doesn't quite know what to do with it!

As for Tom's waistcoat, it's got three armholes instead of two! 'Use one for a leg!' said Amelia with a giggle. But how can he do that?

And now Amelia is knitting the bonnet for the baby doll, but as it is already big enough to go all round the teddy bear's middle, I expect she will have to use it for a shawl!

Can't you be sensible,

Amelia Jane – just for once? Tie her up to the table-leg again, toys! She's just too bad for words.

Oh, Bother Amelia Jane!

'What are you doing, Amelia Jane?' asked the sailor doll. 'What do you want that water for?'

'I'm going to paint,' said Amelia. 'See, I've found a paint-box in the toy-cupboard. I know how to paint because I've watched the children.'

'How do you paint?' asked the sailor doll.

Amelia Jane dipped her paint-brush into the water and then rubbed it on one of the little squares of colour in the paint-box.

'I paint like this!' she said with a giggle and splashed a big stripe of green all across the sailor doll's face!

He was very angry. He went off to

tell the other toys. 'She's in one of her silly moods again,' he said to Tom. 'We'd better look out!'

Amelia Jane painted hard all the morning. At first she painted pictures on a piece of paper. Then she looked round for something better to do with her paints.

'The dolls' house! I'll paint monkeys climbing up the wall,' she said. 'The little dolls have gone out for a walk – they'll be surprised when they come back!'

So she painted little brown monkeys all the way up the front walls of the pretty little dolls' house – they did look peculiar!

The dolls'-house dolls screamed when they came back. 'Look! What's that on the walls? Monkeys! Are they real? Oh, what's happened to our dear little house?'

'You be careful in case there are monkeys inside it too!' said Amelia Jane, and not one of the tiny dolls dared to go in at their front door!

Then she saw the little wooden train standing by itself in a corner of the room. The engine-driver had gone to talk to the teddy bear, so he wasn't there. Amelia Jane took her pot of water and paint-box – and do you know what she did? She painted rows of silly faces all round the engine and its trucks!

'Look! What's happened? Where did these dreadful faces come from?' cried the engine-driver when he saw them. 'My beautiful train! Everyone will laugh at me when I drive it.'

'You'd better get a cloth and rub all the faces off,' said Tom. 'Bother Amelia Jane! I'll help you, Engine-driver.'

So they spent a long, long time trying to get the faces off the engine and the train. They were very hot and tired by the end of it.

'I'd be much obliged if you would go and give Amelia Jane a good telling-off from me,' said the engine-driver. 'I'm too small to do it myself.'

'With pleasure,' said Tom and he went up to Amelia Jane, and gave her a good scolding. She was very angry – and you can guess what she did! She painted his hat white when he was asleep!

It did look strange.

He was very much upset. All the toys stood round him and giggled.

'What happened?' said the teddy bear. 'Your hat's all white, Tom!'

Tom had to climb up to the little wash-basin, turn on a tap, put the plug in, and try to wash the white off his hat. He managed to get himself wet all over, and the white ran down his jacket and trousers.

So then he had to sit in front of the fire, and when his jacket dried it shrank and was so tight that he could hardly breathe. He was very, very cross with Amelia Jane!

She painted the clockwork mouse's tail a bright red, and he thought it was a worm running after him. He raced away, squealing, 'I can't get away from that red worm; it follows me, it follows me!' The toys couldn't help laughing.

'It's only your tail. Don't be afraid of your own tail,' said the bear. 'Go and climb up to the bookshelf, where the bowl of goldfish is. Sit on the edge and dip your tail into the water. The red will run off and you will be all right again.'

'Yes, you do that,' said Amelia Jane, with a grin. *She* knew what would happen, but the others didn't! The clockwork mouse got up on to the bookcase, and went to the goldfish bowl. He sat on the edge and dipped his red tail into the water.

The goldfish were very excited. 'A worm! A lovely long red worm!' they bubbled to one another. 'Quick, catch it and eat it!'

And they swam to the little red tail and snapped at it. Goodness – the mouse almost fell backwards into the water! 'Don't! Don't! That's my tail!' he squealed.

He only just managed to get it out of

the bowl before it was nibbled off. He
raced down to the floor, tumbling over
and over when he got there.

Amelia Jane laughed and laughed.
The clockwork mouse cried bitterly. 'I
wish *you* had a tail!' he said to Amelia
Jane. 'I'd come and nibble it, then you'd
know how it felt!'

Now the next night, a small mouse, a real one this time, came running out of a hole in the playroom wall with a little note in his mouth. It was from the toys in the next house.

'I say!' said the clockwork clown, reading the note. 'The toys next door are giving a fancy dress party! What fun! It's the night after next. Well, *I* shall go as a pirate!'

'I shall go as one of the bears in the story of The Three Bears,' said the teddy bear.

'And I shall make myself a red cloak and hood and go as Red Riding Hood,' said the tiny doll in the corner of the toy-cupboard.

'I shall go as a queen,' said Amelia Jane, grandly. 'I can easily make myself a crown, and there's a beautiful dress laid away in a box in one of the drawers over there. I can make a cloak, and I have got a very pretty necklace that came out of a cracker.'

Well, Amelia Jane worked very hard indeed at making the lovely cloak. It was royal purple and she sewed tiny silver beads all over it, from the bead box. She tried on her crown – how lovely she looked! She put on the necklace.

'Don't I look beautiful?' she said to the other toys. 'I shall win the first prize for the fancy dress. I know I shall!'

Tom thought she probably would.

'You don't deserve to,' he said. 'You've been unkind. The clockwork mouse is still upset because the red hasn't properly come off his tail.'

'Pooh!' said Amelia Jane. 'You wait till I get the paint-box out again. I'll do MUCH worse things than that!'

That made the toys very angry. The bear decided to take the paint-box and hide it when Amelia wasn't looking. It was quite easy to do that because she was so tired that night with her hard work sewing on the silver beads that she fell asleep!

'Look at her – fast asleep!' said Tom. 'She doesn't *deserve* to win the first prize at the party. But she will!'

'She won't,' said the bear, suddenly. 'I've got an idea, Tom. Listen – *I* can paint just as well as Amelia Jane can. And I'm going to paint her face in all kinds of stripes and dots while she's asleep! It'll be red and blue and green and yellow!'

The toys stood and giggled as the bear took the paint-brush, dipped it into the little pot of water, and began to paint Amelia's sleeping face. Goodness, he did it well! Stripes of red and green, dots of blue and yellow, crosses of black and brown.

Oh dear – what a terrifying sight Amelia Jane looked!

'But she'll see herself in the mirror,

won't she?' said the clockwork mouse.

'No, because she would have to climb up on the bookcase, and stand there to see herself in the mirror on the wall,' said the bear. 'And she won't do that when she's wearing a cloak. She couldn't climb in that.'

Well, when Amelia Jane woke up, she didn't know anything about her painted face, of course. All the toys put on fancy dresses for the party – and Amelia Jane couldn't *think* why they giggled every time they looked at her. In fact the clockwork mouse laughed so much that his key fell out.

Amelia walked up and down, wearing her crown and necklace, with the beautiful silk dress going 'swish-swish-swish' all the time, and her cloak flying out behind her, gleaming with silver beads. She didn't know how funny she looked, with her painted face, all stripes and dots and crosses!

'First prize for *me*!' she said to the toys. 'Don't you think so?'

That made them giggle again, of course. Amelia Jane simply couldn't understand them. 'You're being very silly tonight,' she said. 'Well – I'm just going out into the passage to look at myself in the long mirror there. I don't want to climb up to the bookcase mirror in this long cloak.'

The toys had quite forgotten *that* mirror! They wondered whatever Amelia Jane would say when she saw herself. She walked out into the passage – and then she gave a loud scream.

'Oh! OH! My face! What's happened to it? Oh, you wicked bad toys, you've painted it! And I haven't time to wash it off properly. Oh, you horrid mean things.'

'We've only done to you what you did to us!' said Tom, grinning. 'You can't go to the party like that – and it serves you right!'

'I shall come! I shall! You just see!' cried Amelia Jane, and she took off her crown and necklace and began to undo her cloak. 'Yes, and I'll get first prize, too! Oh, you unkind things!'

'Well, we won't wait. It's time we set off,' said the bear. 'Goodbye, Amelia Jane. We are sorry we shan't see you at the fancy dress party.'

But all the same Amelia is going! I look like an Indian, with war-paint on my face! she thought, as she threw off her lovely dress. All right – I'll go as an Indian! Where's that little shuttle-cock with coloured feathers set round it? They will do for my hair!

She pulled out the feathers and set them round her head. Then she looked for the little wigwam tent that the bear and Tom sometimes played with. It was painted brightly.

'That will do for a cloak,' said Amelia. 'And where's that rubber axe? Ah, here it is – that shall be my tomahawk! And who shall be my enemies? The toy soldier, the bear and all the rest! Look out – I'm coming to the party after all!'

And off she went at top speed, the

fiercest Indian you ever saw. What a shock the toys are going to get! I can only hope that naughty Amelia Jane doesn't win the first prize after all!

Goodbye,
Amelia Jane!

The toys played a trick on Amelia Jane the other day.

Amelia Jane was always playing tricks on all the toys in the nursery. There was no end to her mischief. If she didn't think of one thing, she thought of another.

There was the time when she

collected worms in the garden and popped them all into Tom's shut umbrella. They wriggled about there and couldn't get out, poor things.

And then Amelia sent Tom out into the garden to fetch her hanky from the garden seat. It was raining, of course, so she gave him his umbrella.

'Better put this up,' she said, and he did. And out slithered all the worms, on top of his head and down his neck, as soon as he got out into the garden in the rain.

The worms fled into holes very

thankfully, but Tom got such a fright
that he ran straight into the pond and
got wet through.

He was very, very angry with Amelia
Jane, but she only laughed.

'You shouldn't let worms nest in your
umbrella,' she said.

Another time,
Amelia took the
teapot out of the
toy tea-set
and
filled it with
hot water
from the
tap.
Then

she climbed up to the roof of the dolls' house and poured the hot water down the chimney.

The little dolls'-house dolls rushed out of the front door in fright, with water trickling down the stairs after them, and Amelia Jane nearly fell off the roof with laughing.

She was well scolded for that bit of mischief, but she wouldn't even say she was sorry.

The toys had a meeting about her.

'I'm tired of Amelia Jane,' said the toy soldier.

'So am I,' said the clockwork clown. 'She took my key away yesterday for about the fiftieth time.'

'Can't we get rid of her?' said the teddy bear.

'We've often tried,' said the clockwork mouse. 'But we never have.'

'I've got an idea,' said Tom, his eyes shining brightly. 'It's a small idea at the moment – but if we talk about it, it might grow into a big one and be really good.'

'What is it?' asked the clockwork clown.

'Well – you know you can slide down the stairs on a tray, don't you?' said Tom.

Everyone nodded.

'That's my idea,' said Tom. 'It's only just that. I haven't thought any more than that.'

'It seems rather silly,' said the bear. 'Did you mean to get Amelia Jane to slide down the stairs on a tray, or what?'

'I don't know,' said Tom. 'I tell you, I hadn't thought any further than I said.'

'Ooooh!' said the clown. '*Could* we make her slide down on a tray – push her very, very hard . . . ?'

'And have the front door open so that she shot right out in a hurry,' went on the bear.

'And have the garden gate open so that she'd shoot out there, too,' said the clown.

'And then down the hill she'd go, whizz-bang, faster and faster and faster,' said the clockwork mouse, excitedly.

'And splash into the stream on her tray, and off it would go like a boat, all the way down to the sea!' finished Tom, his face beaming with excitement.

'And we'd never, never see her again, the bad, naughty doll,' said the bear.

'No, we wouldn't. We'd shout, "Goodbye, Amelia Jane!" when she flew out of the front door, and that would be that,' said Tom. 'See what my little idea has grown to – a great big one. I thought it would!'

Well, the toys talked and talked about their idea, and got very excited about it indeed. Surely they could at last get rid of that naughty Amelia Jane!

Amelia didn't know anything about all this, of course. She was out in the garden collecting a few more worms to play another trick. Tom had time to get out the big tin tray from its corner and rub soap underneath it to make it more slippery.

'We'll play our trick when everyone is out tomorrow,' he decided. 'If I stand on a chair in the hall I can open the front door all right. Now, don't say a word about our plan, any of you!'

The next afternoon the house was very quiet because everyone had gone out. Tom took the tin tray and banged hard on it. 'Boom, diddy-boom!'

'Stop that noise,' said Amelia Jane,

crossly. 'I want to have a snooze.'

'All right. Have one,' said Tom. 'We are all going to the top of the stairs to play at sliding down on this tea-tray. We'll have a lovely time – and we don't want *you*, Amelia Jane!'

Well, that was quite enough to make Amelia want to come, of course! 'I'm coming, too,' she said. 'And I guess I'll go faster down the stairs than any of you!'

Off they all went to the top of the stairs. Tom ran down, got a chair, stood on it, and opened the front door. He ran back and had his turn at sliding down. The tray went down to the bottom, bumpity-bumpity-bump, slid a little way down the hall and stopped. Aha! If they all pushed hard when Amelia Jane had her turn, it would most certainly fly out of the door, down the path, out of the gate and away down the hill to the stream at the bottom!

'I want my turn, I want mine!' shouted Amelia, and she got on to the tray. She held tight – and the toy soldier, the bear, the clockwork clown, the mouse and another doll all pushed as hard as ever they could.

Whoooooosh! You should have seen that tray fly down the stairs at top speed! Amelia's breath was quite taken away. Her hair and her dress flew out behind her, and she stared in fright. This

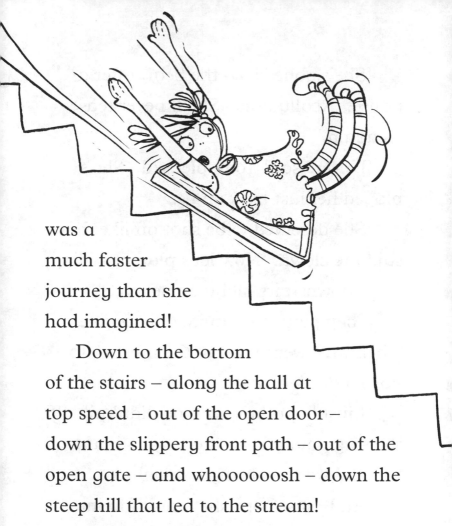

was a
much faster
journey than she
had imagined!

Down to the bottom
of the stairs – along the hall at
top speed – out of the open door –
down the slippery front path – out of the
open gate – and whoooooosh – down the
steep hill that led to the stream!

'Goodbye, Amelia Jane!' shouted the
toys. 'Goodbye, goodbye!'

'She's gone,' said the bear, after a pause. 'Really gone. She'll never tease us again.'

'Never,' said Tom, pleased. 'She's played her last trick on us.'

'She deserved to be shot off like that,' said the clown. 'Now let's play at sliding trays downstairs all by ourselves.'

They played for quite a long time. Then they went back to the nursery to have a drink of water.

'I just hope Amelia Jane didn't tip off the tray going down the hill, and hurt herself,' said the bear, suddenly.

'And I just hope she didn't fall into the stream and get drowned,' said the clown.

'It seems a bit funny without her,' said the mouse. 'Er – you don't suppose we were dreadfully unkind, do you?'

'Not a bit,' said Tom. 'She deserved to be sent off like that.'

'But you wouldn't want her to hurt herself, would you?' said the bear, solemnly. 'You know – I keep on and on thinking what would happen if she tipped off the tray going down-hill – suppose she fell under a bus – or . . .'

The clockwork mouse gave a squeal of fright. 'Don't say things like that. They frighten me. You make me feel as if I want Amelia Jane back.'

'Perhaps she wasn't as bad as she seemed,' said the bear. 'You know – I don't feel very nice about playing that trick on her now. I feel sort of uncomfortable.'

'Pooh!' said Tom, but he didn't say any more.

Well, what *had* happened to Amelia Jane? She had slid out into the front garden and out of the gate, and down the hill at top speed. She was very frightened indeed. Why had the toys shouted goodbye? Was it a trick they had played on her to get rid of her? Amelia Jane wailed aloud as she shot down the hill. Oh dear, oh dear, had she been so dreadful that the toys wanted to get rid of her like that?

'I'm going straight into the stream!'

she squealed, and splash, into the water she went. She clung to the tray. It didn't sink, but bobbed on the surface, with a very wet Amelia Jane clinging on top. Down the stream she went, bobbing on the waves.

She floated for a very long way. Then the tray bumped into the bank, stuck into some weeds and stopped. Amelia thankfully crawled off on to the land. She was wet and cold and tired. She could see a dog not far off and she was frightened of him.

Where could she hide? What was that lying on the grass over there? A bicycle! It had a basket behind the saddle, and Amelia Jane staggered off to it. She squeezed into the basket, and stuffed an old bit of newspaper over herself. Now, perhaps, nobody, not even the dog, would see her.

She fell asleep and dreamed of the toys. She dreamt that they were all cross with her, and she cried in her sleep.

'Don't be cross with me. I'll be good, I'll be good.'

Then she woke up – and dear me, she was wobbling from side to side in the basket. Somebody had picked up the bicycle, mounted it, and was now riding away down the river path – with Amelia Jane tucked into the basket at the back.

Oh, dear! thought Amelia, in a panic. 'Now where am I going? I'm miles and miles away from home – and from all the toys. I wish I was back again. Wouldn't I be good if I could only get back to the nursery! But the toys wouldn't be pleased to see me at all. They'd turn me out again.'

On she went and on. Miles and miles it seemed to Amelia Jane, and she grew cramped and cold in the basket. And then, at last, the rider stopped and jumped off.

He flung his bicycle against something, and walked off, whistling.

Amelia Jane peeped out. The bicycle was against a wall near a back door. She crawled out of the basket, and almost fell to the ground. She ran to the door. If only she could get into a house, she could hide.

In she went, and somebody jumped in surprise as the big doll ran past. Amelia tore into the hall and up the stairs. She almost fell inside a room, and stopped there, panting in fright.

And will you believe it, she was back in the nursery again – and there were all the toys she knew, staring at her in amazement – the toy soldier, the bear, the clown, the mouse and everyone!

She had come all the way home in the basket of the bicycle belonging to one of the children! He had gone to the river that day, and then had cycled all the way back – and Amelia Jane was in his basket. What a very, very peculiar thing!

'You said goodbye to me – but here I am again,' said Amelia, in a funny, shaky sort of voice. 'It seems as if you c-c-c-can't get rid of me!'

She burst into tears – and then everyone ran to comfort her. She was patted and fussed, and even Tom kept saying he was glad to see her back.

'Oh, dear – this is all so nice,' said Amelia at last. 'I won't be mischievous again, toys. I won't play tricks any more. I'll be just as good as gold!'

'We don't believe you,' said Tom. 'But never mind – we're glad to have you back, you bad, naughty doll. We

never *really* want to say goodbye to you,
Amelia Jane!'

I don't either. What about you?